D0569080

WHAT A YEAR IT WAS!
1947

A walk back in time to revisit
what life was like in the year that
has special meaning for you...

Congratulations
and
Best Wishes

To

From

DEDICATION

*To Kenny Bookbinder, Whose Support And Commitment
To This Project Helped Keep It Alive.*

Designer • Peter Hess
Researcher • Laurie Cohn

Text and images Copyright ©1996 by Beverly Cohn.
Compilation copyright ©1996 by MMS Publishing. All rights reserved under international
copyright conventions. No part of this book may be reproduced or utilized in any form or by
any means, electronic or mechanical, including photocopying, recording, or by any
information storage and retrieval system, without permission in writing from the publisher.
Inquiries should be addressed to:
MMS Publishing, 330 Washington Boulevard, Suite 611, Marina del Rey, California 90292.
Printed and bound in the United States.

CONTENTS

POLITICS & WORLD EVENTS

"I have issued a proclamation terminating the period of hostilities of World War II as of 12:00 o'clock Noon December 31, 1946. While the law of numerous wartime emergency statutes ceased to be effective upon the issuance of this proclamation. It is my belief that the time has come when such a declaration can be properly made and that it is the public interest to make it. Most of the powers effected by the proclamation need longer need to be exercised by the executive branch of the government. This is entirely in keeping with the policies which I have consistently followed in an effort to bring our economy and government back to a peacetime basis as quickly as possible."

President Truman Signs Proclamation Formally Ending World War II.

CAPITAL HILL

J oe Martin becomes the first Republican Speaker Of The House since 1931.

Capital Hill Is Once Again The Nation's Focal Point As The 80th Congress Convenes During One Of The Most Crucial Periods In The Nation's History.

WHAT A YEAR IT WAS!

Speaker Martin swears in the 430 new members of the House.

President Truman shakes hands with Senator Vandenberg, President Pro Tem of the Senate and Speaker Martin, handing them each a copy of his address.

President Truman delivers his State Of The Union to the Joint Session of Congress, which is heavily weighed by the opposition.

SECRETARIES OF STATE

James F. Byrnes

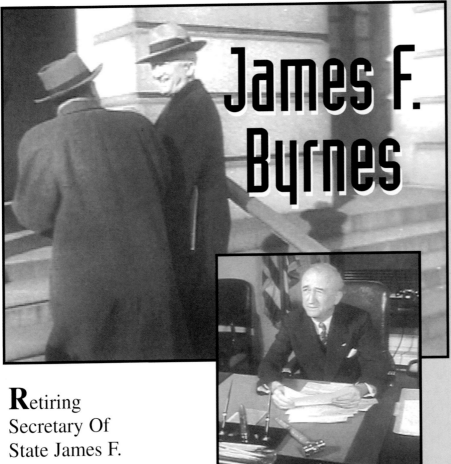

Retiring Secretary Of State James F. Byrnes arrives at the State Department after handing his resignation to President Truman because of failing health.

Secretary Byrnes established a brilliant record of public service. His leadership in the peace conferences and in guiding our policy in the United Nations will be chronicled by future historians. The nation owes him a debt of eternal gratitude.

General George C. Marshall is sworn in as Secretary Of State by Chief Justice Vincent succeeding retiring James F. Byrnes.

WHAT A YEAR IT WAS!

General George C. Marshall

Photographers capture this historic moment for their newspapers.

Shaking hands with President Truman, the new Secretary of State is next in line for the Presidency since there is no Vice-President

The former Chief of Staff and Envoy to China receives good luck wishes from his friend Jimmy Byrnes.

NEW CONGRESS PERSONALITIES

THE REPUBLICANS HOLD A CAUCUS AS THE NATION'S 80TH CONGRESS PREPARES TO CONVENE.

Senator Arthur Vandenberg presides and is nominated President Pro Tem of the Senate.

The Republicans, boasting a majority for the first time in fourteen years, are lead by Senator Taft (center) pictured with Senators Markman (left) and Bridges (right).

WHAT A YEAR IT WAS!

Senator Taft is the leading Republican presidential possibility.

Majority Leader Senator White of Maine.

Senator Bricker of Ohio announces he will back Taft for presidential nomination.

Henry Cabot Lodge (rt.), pictured with Senator Cooper of Kentucky, attends caucus having returned from the war.

TRUMAN RECEIVES HONORARY DEGREE

Truman Names Lewis W. Douglas Ambassador To Great Britain.

President Truman In Canada On First Official State Visit By An American President.

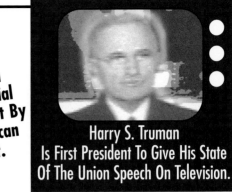

Harry S. Truman Is First President To Give His State Of The Union Speech On Television.

Returning from Mexico, President Truman stops at Waco, Texas where he receives an Honorary Degree Of Doctor Of Law from Baylor University.

Truman Predicts U.S. Government Will End Fiscal Year With Record Surplus of $4.7 Billion Which Will Be Used To Reduce The National Debt.

Truman Vetoes Republican Bill To Cut Income Taxes Insisting Any Surplus Should Be Applied To Reduction Of National Debt Which He Reduces By Over $11 Billion Dollars, First Downturn In 17 Years.

The President Takes A Strong Stand On International Trade.

"We are the giants of the economic world. Whether we like it or not the future pattern of economic relations depends upon us. The world is waiting and watching to see what we shall do. The choice is ours. We can lead the nations to economic peace or we can plunge them into economic war. There must be no question as to our course. We must not go through the 30's again."

Harry Truman
Quips:
"If he knew what it entails, no man in his right mind would ever want to be President..."

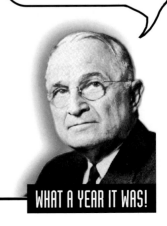

WHAT A YEAR IT WAS!

THE NATIONAL SECURITY ACT PROVIDES FOR THE FOLLOWING:

• REGROUPS THE ARMED FORCES INTO A NATIONAL MILITARY ESTABLISHMENT;

• ESTABLISHES THE NATIONAL SECURITY COUNCIL WHICH ADVISES THE PRESIDENT ON MATTERS PERTAINING TO NATIONAL SECURITY;

• CREATES THE CENTRAL INTELLIGENCE AGENCY (CIA) WHOSE FUNCTION IS TO COORDINATE AND ANALYZE FOREIGN INTELLIGENCE REPORTS FOR THE PRESIDENT TO WHOM THE AGENCY IS DIRECTLY ACCOUNTABLE. IT IS MANDATED THAT IN ORDER TO PROTECT AMERICAN CITIZENS, THE CIA IS FORBIDDEN ANY INVOLVEMENT IN DOMESTIC SECURITY MATTERS.

THE NATIONAL SECURITY ACT ESTABLISHES A DEPARTMENT OF THE ARMY, DEPARTMENT OF THE NAVY AND A DEPARTMENT OF THE AIR FORCE WITHIN THE DEPARTMENT OF DEFENSE.

The Navy Organizes Its First Underwater Offensive Strike Units Called The Underwater Demolition Teams.

Under An Amended U.S. Presidential Act, The Presidency Goes To The Speaker Of The House In The Absence Of A Vice-President With The President Pro Tem Of The Senate And Secretary Of State Next In Succession Followed By Members Of The Cabinet.

The 22nd Amendment Approved By Congress Limits The Term Of The U.S. Presidency To Two Full Terms.

A Session Of The House Of Representatives Is Televised For The First Time.

The U.S. Begins Broadcasting Information On The U.S. To The Soviet People.

The General Agreement On Tariffs And Trade Is Passed.

Republicans Control Both Houses Of Congress For The First Time In 16 Years.

Freshman Senator:
• Joseph McCarthy (Rep. Wisconsin)

Freshman Congressmen:
• John F. Kennedy (Dem. Mass.)
• Richard M. Nixon (Rep. Calif.)

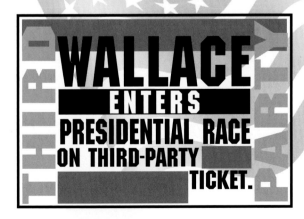

WALLACE ENTERS PRESIDENTIAL RACE ON THIRD-PARTY TICKET.

REPUBLICANS

An Average Guy with an eye to the

Future

Going Places in the <u>New</u> National Guard Today

Join thousands of alert young men in the *new* National Guard, earn from $1.25 per hour up for training in your spare time. Prepare for a better civilian job. Enjoy modern athletic facilities! Fly in the latest planes or use modern ground equipment!

Veterans can probably obtain rank held upon discharge. And now, young men 17 years old may join the National Guard.

For complete information about the National Guard unit in your community, contact the officers of that unit or write to the Adjutant General of your state.

He's a veteran of World War II, served overseas 2 years, was honorably discharged as a buck sergeant. Thought his outfit was the best in the service.

Married, has one child, a steady job with good pay. Rents now, plans to buy home later. Extra National Guard pay helps wife balance their budget.

Likes sports, plays on National Guard indoor baseball and basketball teams. Studies in spare time to help further his chances in his civilian occupation.

Wife likes dancing. They get a sitter, go to most National Guard dances. Evening costs little. They enjoy "getting out" with their many friends.

Employer is old Guardsman, has agreed to let him go to summer camp where he gets full military pay and allowances. He has a regular vacation, too.

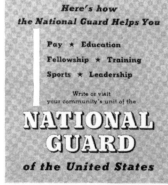

Here's how the National Guard Helps You

Pay ★ Education
Fellowship ★ Training
Sports ★ Leadership

Write or visit your community's unit of the

NATIONAL GUARD of the United States

Listen to "On Stage America" starring Paul Whiteman, every Monday, 9 P.M., EST, ABC network . . . and "First Call" with Martin Block and Ray Bloch, every Thursday, 9:30 P.M., EST, Mutual network.

LEWIS DOUGLAS

Newly appointed Ambassador to England Lewis Douglas pays a visit to President Truman at the White House.

Douglas being sworn in.

Dean Atchinson, acting Secretary of State, congratulates Ambassador Lewis.

General of the Army and Chief of Staff Eisenhower visits with G.I. patients in a hospital in Florida.

IKE DENIES POLITICAL AMBITIONS

In Florida for a vacation and medical check up, Ike holds his first all-out press conference since coming south, denying any political ambitions.

WHAT A YEAR IT WAS!

Several hundred miles offshore, a German B-2 rocket is prepared for test launching.

The rocket is successfully launched and opens up a new chapter in sea warfare.

U.S CELEBRATES NAVY DAY

This is the first launching of a heavy bombardment rocket from a moving platform.

WHAT A YEAR IT WAS!

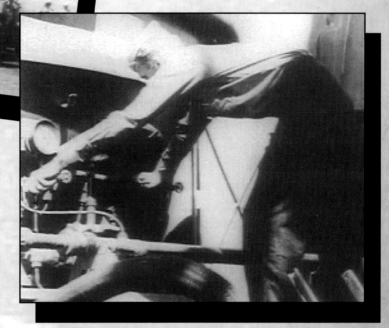

A huge liquid oxygen tank is brought topside from the hangar deck

The U.S. Carrier Midway Gets Ready For A Firing Operation.

The fuel is piped into the big rocket.

A fire control gang stands by in case of an emergency.

1947

Despite Loud Protesting Inside The "Gallery Of Peace" At The French Foreign Ministry, The Allied Nations (United States, Canada, Britain, France And The USSR) Formally Terminate State Of War With Axis Powers (Italy, Finland, Rumania, Bulgaria And Hungary) And Sign Peace Treaties.

The United States Signs 99-Year Treaty With The Philippines Guaranteeing Presence Of American Military And Naval Bases.

The United States Condemns The Nationalist And Communist Chinese Governments And Withdraws As Mediator. Convinced That The Only Way To Deal With The Communists Is By Brute Force, Chiang Kai-Shek Blames America For The Chinese Civil War Claiming That If President Truman Armed The Nationalists, The War With The Communists Could Have Been Averted.

Washington Denounces The Soviets On Their Interference In The Internal Affairs Of Hungary. Premier Nagy Forced Into Exile. U.S. Suspends $15 Million Credit To The Hungarian Government Pending Further Investigations.

27 Belgian Collaborators Executed In Dinan, France.

The United Nations Calls On Dutch And Indonesians To Halt Java War.

Egyptians Riot Against The U.N. In Cairo.

Sugar Rationing Ends In The U.S.

A.F.L. Accuses Juan Peron Of Using Army To Establish Dictatorship Over Argentine Labor.

President Truman Addresses Congress With Proposal To Send Aid To Greece And Turkey To Help In War Recovery And To Strengthen Freedom. $400 Million In Aid Is Approved.

Franco Elected By 80% Of The Vote In Spain's Elections.

Associated Press Correspondent Jack Guinn Expelled From Hungary On Charges Of Spying.

French Troops Suppress Rebellion In Cambodia.

Communists And Socialists Gain Majority Hold Through Rigged Elections In Poland.

Greek Army Stems Drive Of 2,500 Guerrillas On Yanina.

U.S. Rushes Grain To West Germany To Help Restore Civil Unrest And Food Strikes.

James Forrestal Becomes First American Secretary Of Defense.

The U.S. And USSR Voice Support For Palestine Partition.

Marshall Warns Soviets To Stop "Brazen" Propaganda Attacks Against The United States.

France Elects Vincent Auriol As President.

Nazi Germany Divided Into Four Zones Of Occupation By Victorious Allies.

Soviets Refuse U.S. Inspection Of Hungarian Army.

Great Britain And France Sign Alliance Treaty.

Jewish Agency For Palestine Accepts Proposed Partition Of The Holy Land At Session Of The United Nations.

16 European Nations, Not Including Communist Countries, Meet In Paris To Discuss The Marshall Plan.

Bloody Religious Wars Between Hindus And Moslems Spread To All Major Indian Cities

Burma Premier And Five Aides Assassinated In Rangoon.

Egypt Asks The United Nations To End British Control Of The Sudan.

Gandhi's House Stoned As Riots Sweep Lahore In Punjab.

Burma Becomes Independent Republic.

British Plan For Partition Of India Accepted By India Congress.

Andrei A. Gromyko, Soviet Representative On The United Nations' Security Council, Vehemently Objects To The Atomic Policy Plan Developed By Bernard Baruch Calling For International Controls Of The Crucial Stages Of Atomic Production Rather Than Allowing Each Country To Develop Its Own Capabilities. In A Bitter Speech, Gromyko Claims That Such Interference Would Imperil National Independence.

Britain Tries To Solve Labor Shortage In Britain By Enlisting 20,000 Refugee Women From Germany's U.S. Zone.

That extra something that makes "going by Clipper" a delightful experience _____

A Great Tradition Makes You Our Guest

We of Pan American share in a nineteen-year record of public service unequaled in air transport.

We realize and *know in detail* every one of the requirements which make traveling abroad so different from traveling inside the United States—*and so much more interesting!* It is our privilege and duty to act as your host from the minute you reach the airport until you leave us at your destination.

Call on us for help with customs, foreign exchange and immigration procedures — for any personal service great or small regarding your transportation . . . A great tradition makes you our guest.

On foreign soil you're greeted by a friendly Passenger-

"We felt the lure of Latin America the instant we boarded the Clipper"

"'**Sí, Señores Ramírez,**' the stewardess was saying as we stepped aboard the Clipper . . . '*¿En qué puedo servirles?*'

". . . And the answer of our Latin American fellow passengers was so rapid, so musical, so *different* from English that Tom and I felt we were already in Latin America even before the Clipper took off!

"Here we were at New York in the dead of winter. Yet in only 8 hours, the same stewardess told us in English, we'd be landing in tropical Puerto Rico. . . . Believe it or not, that's almost *a third of the way* to distant Rio de Janeiro!"

January and February are Midsummer in Rio! Here at world-famous Copacabana Beach you can stroll, hatless, along hand-set mosaic sidewalks and laugh at ice and snow. Pan American, the world's most experienced international airline, has made possible a new, more exciting kind of winter vacation in distant foreign lands.

Want to fly somewhere closer to home? Ask your Travel Agent about Clipper service to MEXICO and GUATEMALA! In Guatemala (above) Indian craftsmen weave intricate designs by hand, *without even using a pattern.* You can fly there from Miami, New Orleans, Nuevo Laredo, Houston, Brownsville or Los Angeles . . . Winter is the "dry season" in Guatemala—sunshine every day. Stopovers easily arranged.

Service-Representative who speaks English, makes you feel at home abroad.

PAN AMERICAN WORLD AIRWAYS

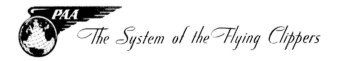

The System of the Flying Clippers

See your local Travel Agent or the nearest Pan American office for rates and reservations, not only to Latin America but also to Europe . . . Africa . . . Alaska . . . Australasia . . . or the Orient.

WORLD'S MOST EXPERIENCED AIRLINE

21

1947

COMMIES, COMMIES, EVERYWHERE

☞ 800 Federal Employees Discharged For Being "Disloyal" Following Secret Investigation Into Communist Affiliation. A Dozen States Ban The Communist Party From Appearing On Election Ballots.

☞ The House Committee On Un-American Activities (HUAC) Begins Hearings On Methods Of Restricting Communist Activities.

☞ Although Agreeing That Communists Are "A Fifth Column..." FBI Director J. Edgar Hoover Recommends Against Outlawing The Party Fearing The Reds Will Go Underground.

☞ Attorney General Tom Clark Begins Prosecuting Communists As Unregistered Foreign Agents.

Hungarian Communists Become Largest Single Party With 21.6% Of The Vote.

Brazil Outlaws Communist Party.

Bernard Baruch Testifies Before Congress That Soviet Spies May Have Infiltrated American Atomic Plants In Canada And Stole Atomic Bomb Secrets.

A United Negro College Fund Report On Negro* Representation In The Professions Reveals The Following Statistics:

▌ **1,000 out of 176,000 lawyers are Negroes*;**

▌ **8,000 out of 400,000 nurses are Negroes*;**

▌ **1 Negro* doctor for every 4,000 Negroes*.**

*Negro was the commonly-used term in 1947.

CIVIL RIGHTS

President Truman's Committee On Civil Rights Recommends Protective Measures To Protect Civil Rights And End Segregation Including The Following:

■ **Federal Anti-Lynching Bill;**

■ **Elimination Of Poll Taxes;**

■ **Removal Of Racial Housing Restrictions;**

■ **Creation Of A Permanent Federal Commission On Civil Rights;**

■ **Reorganization Of The Civil Rights Division Of The Department Of Justice.**

Exodus

1947

BRITISH REFUSE POLITICAL ASYLUM IN PALESTINE TO 4,530 JEWISH REFUGEES FROM GERMANY

Calling them displaced persons and illegal immigrants, Great Britain refuses 4,530 exhausted survivors of the Holocaust entry into the Promised Land. Arriving in the port of Haifa on a ship named "Exodus," the British, with threats of returning the Jews to Germany, force the "Exodus" to return to French waters. The refugees debark in Hamburg after refusing to enter France.

NOVEMBER 29th:
The United Nations Announces Plans To Divide Palestine Into Arab And Jewish States With Full Independence By October 1, 1948 Thus Creating A Permanent Jewish State And Homeland For Survivors Of The Holocaust. Rejecting The Partition, Dr. Hussein Khalidi, Head Of The Palestine Arab High Committee, Threatens An Inevitable Crusade Against The Jews. Star Of David Flags Wave In Jerusalem As Thousands Of Jubilant Jews Sing And Dance In The Streets In Celebration Of A 2,000 Year Dream – A Jewish Homeland.

Jewish Agency Refuses To Aid Great Britain In Apprehending Jewish "Terrorists." In Retaliation, More Than A Third Of Palestine Is Placed Under Martial Law.

Moscow Announces 809,532 German Soldiers Being Held In The USSR.

In A Joint Effort, U.S. And British Operatives Arrest Hundreds Of Organizers Of The Nazi Underground.

Franz von Papen Sentenced In Nuremberg To Eight Years In A Labor Camp For War Crimes.

Rudolf Hess, Former Auschwitz Commandant, Is Hanged In Poland On The Site Of The Concentration Camp.

A U.S. Military Government Tribunal In Nuremberg Indicts 13 High Nazi Generals On Charges Of War Crimes And Crimes Against Humanity.

Highly respected in U. S. Occupied Germany are the colorfully outfitted men of the Constabulary, mobile and vigilant Army Ground Force.

Jig's up, Jerry!

Soon, all missing SS men and their henchmen will be routed from their "haystacks"—routed sternly, but without the vindictiveness which makes victories short-lived. Action — swift, effective and just — stalks every threat to civil and military security in American-occupied Germany.

Charged with this vital job is the U. S. Army's crack Constabulary, a recently organized force of 32,000 hand-picked men, many of them veterans of wartime combat on German soil.

The aims and responsibilities of the Constabulary are without precedent. Its vigilant patrols must squelch riots, smother crime and the black market, back military government orders, patrol frontiers of the U. S. Zone.

Nothing has been spared to make this the best staffed, best dressed, best equipped ground force an army could produce. Many of its men have been decorated. The latest light tanks, armored cars, jeeps, motorcycles and "spotter" planes can whisk at least fifty men to any corner of the Zone within 35 minutes of a call. In four hours, a whole regiment can be on hand!

The Constabulary, and its successful counterparts in Japan and Korea, answer a specialized problem—planned to succeed where other occupation forces throughout the centuries have failed. For, coupled with vigilance and force, is *justice* — a sense of fair play toward the innocent, and of democratic inspiration to young children.

This modernization of ideas, methods and equipment is going on throughout your new Regular Army. It is a sign of the times, on the road to lasting peace. It is the spirit which has attracted over a million young men into the largest volunteer army the world has ever known.

A 3-year enlistment entitles you to choose your favorite branch of service from those still open. High "take-home" pay, the chance to take part in a job that's making history, and many other advantages make an Army career a good bet! Get full details at your Army Recruiting Station.

Listen to "Sound Off," "Warriors of Peace," "Voice of the Army" and "Proudly We Hail" on your radio.

U. S. ARMY RECRUITING SERVICE

YOUR REGULAR ARMY SERVES THE NATION AND MANKIND IN WAR AND PEACE — CHOOSE THIS FINE PROFESSION NOW

24

JAPAN
Retains Right To Fly Rising-Sun Flag.

● **Canadian Liberals Force Ottawa To Cancel Deportation Of Canadian-Japanese Citizens.**

● **U.N. Council Votes U.S. Trusteeship Of Japanese Pacific Isles As USSR And Great Britain Give In.**

● **The First Gubernatorial Election Is Carried Out In Japan As The Constitution Of Japan Comes Into Force.**

India Abolishes "UNTOUCHABILITY" In Any Form.

Ferenc Nagy
Ousted As Hungary's Premier While Vacationing In Switzerland And Is Replaced By Pro-Soviet Lajos Dinnyes.

CZECHS & POLES Sign 20-Year Mutual Aid Pact In Warsaw.

ETHIOPIA
Declines U.N. Aid On Grounds That Other Countries Are In Greater Need Of Help.

Out Of India
Former World War II Hero Lord Mountbatten, The New Viceroy Of India, Arrives In New Delhi To The Delight Of Indian Leaders.

India Partitioned Into India And Pakistan.

Great Britain Pledges To Withdraw From India By June 1948.

MIDDLE EAST EVENTS

MIDDLE

JANUARY

■ Truce In Palestine Is Broken Between The Jewish Underground And British Military After Underground Blows Up Haifa District Police Station.

■ In A Move To Combat The Jewish Underground, Evacuation Of British Women And Children From Palestine Ordered By Lt. General Sir Alan G. Cunningham.

FEBRUARY

■ The Jewish Underground Vows To Fight To Its Last Breath As Jewish National Council Turns Down British Demand For Help In Smashing The Underground.

■ Arab Delegates In London Turn Down British Compromise Proposal For Settling The Arab-Jewish Problem.

■ British Foreign Secretary Bevin Announces That Britain Cannot Solve The Palestine Problem And Is Turning It Over To The United Nations.

■ Jewish Underground In Palestine Cuts Oil Pipe Lines And Stages Mortar And Machine-Gun Attack Against Royal Air Force Field.

MARCH

■ Jewish Underground Attacks British Installation And Bombs British Officers' Club.

■ Winston Churchill Urges British Government To Seek Solutions To The Palestine Problem To End Warfare In The Holy Land.

■ Jewish Underground Defies British Martial Law And Stages Attacks On Army And Police Centers In Tel Aviv.

APRIL

■ Arab Proposal To Have The U.N. General Assembly Rule On Palestine Independence Is Rejected 8-1 By Assembly's General Committee.

MAY

■ U.N. General Assembly Rejects Arab Proposal To Discuss Termination Of British Mandate And Independence Of Palestine.

■ Jewish Terrorists Blast Their Way Into A Palestine Prison Freeing 251 Prisoners – 120 Jews And 131 Arabs.

■ U.N. General Assembly Inquiry To Exclude All Reference To Independence Of Palestine By 29-14 Vote.

■ U.N. General Assembly Establishes 11-Nation Committee Of Inquiry Into Palestine Question And Urges Palestinians To Cease Violence Pending Decision.

■ Irgun, Jewish Underground Force, Agrees To Truce If British Forces Also Stop Fighting.

JUNE

■ Swedish Jurist, Emil Sandstroem, Elected Chairman Of U.N. Committee Of Inquiry On Palestine.

WHAT A YEAR IT WAS!

EAST

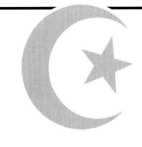

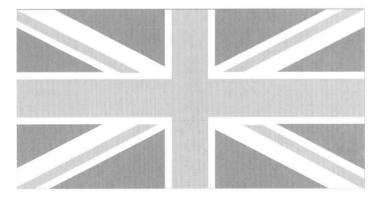

JULY

■ A Jewish Agency Spokesman Testifies Before The U.N. Inquiry Committee That Britain Deliberately Obstructed The Growth Of Jewish Industry And Exploited Jewish Palestine.

SEPTEMBER

■ Britain Announces Its Decision To End Its Palestine Mandate To The U.N. General Assembly's Committee On Palestine.

■ Spokesman For The Arab Higher Committee Told U.S. Special Committee On Palestine That Arabs In The Holy Land Will Not Accept Partition.

OCTOBER

■ Herschel V. Johnson, U.S. Representative On U.N. General Assembly's Palestine Committee, Endorses Partition And Suggests A Special Constabulary To Keep Order In The Holy Land.

NOVEMBER

■ The U.S. And The Soviets Endorse New U.N. Partition Plan After Reaching A Compromise. Britain To End Its Mandate And Military Occupation By May 1, 1948.

■ Britain Begins Withdrawal Of Forces From Palestine.

■ U.N. General Assembly Approves By 33-13 Vote Proposal To Divide Palestine Into Arab And Jewish States Both To Achieve Full Independence By October 1, 1948. Zionists Express Joy While The Arabs Express Bitterness.

DECEMBER

■ Violence Breaks Out In Jerusalem As Arabs Battle With Haganah, Zionist Defense Army. Arab World Called Upon By Moslem Holy Men To Start A Holy War Against Partition.

■ 44 People Die In Out-Break Of Violence In Aden.

EVENTS

REBELLION FLARES IN INDO-CHINA

French troops clear the outskirts of Hanoi after a several week siege by the Vietnamese leaving burning homes in the wake of their destruction.

The city, attacked by rebels following the breakdown of negotiations for independence, was cut off in a lightning attack.

Retreating insurgents leave a trail of fire as they flee before French colonel forces heavily reinforced by units of the Foreign Legion.

Snipers are hunted down through the burning streets.

FRANÇAIS

A BAS LA POLITIQUE

The retreating troops leave their slogans – DOWN WITH FRENCH RULE

Jeeps rush help as mopping operations proceed.

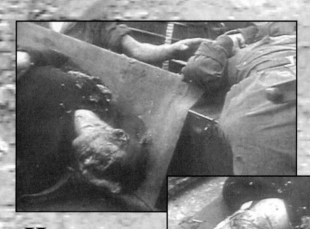

Hundreds of casualties on both sides fall as the fight for Hanoi takes on the proportions of a major engagement.

Evidence of Japanese equipment used by the Vietnamese is this Japanese helmet.

"... HE ASKED ME WHAT OIL *I* USE"

There he goes... happy as a clam. I told him I use Macmillan Ring-Free Motor Oil... just like 3 out of 5 of us independent dealers* throughout the country.

"That's for me!" said Kilroy. I'll take the oil you experts choose."

Everybody's getting in on the act! Seems like all my customers are going for the oil the experts use. No wonder! It's different... refined by an exclusive, patented process ...guaranteed to *clean as it lubricates!* There's no other oil just like it.

Here's my shingle .... and you'll find it on highways and side streets all over the country. Wherever you see the red Macmillan sign, you'll find an independent dealer... an oil expert. Drive in. Ask him. Follow his advice. Make yours Macmillan, too.

Throughout the nation *3 out of 5* of these dealers* say:

"*I USE MACMILLAN IN MY CAR!*"

⬛ MACMILLAN PET. CORP. 1947

Thousands of independent dealers who sell Macmillan and more than 800 other brands of oil.

PRINCESS ELIZABETH,

HEIR TO ENGLISH THRONE, MARRIES PHILIP MOUNTBATTEN, DUKE OF EDINBURGH, AT WESTMINSTER ABBEY.

In a ceremony filled with pomp and circumstance, Princess Elizabeth, daughter of King George VI and Queen Elizabeth, wed her dashingly handsome cousin, Prince Philip. Thousands of well-wishers line the procession route cheering the royal entourage.

NOBEL PEACE PRIZE

Friends Service Council (Britain)
American Friends Service Committee

ARRIVALS:
HILLARY CLINTON

P A S S I N G S

JACQUES-PHILIPPE LECLERC, French General And War Hero Who Liberated France, Dies At 45.

VICTOR EMMANUEL III, Ex-King Of Italy, Dies At 78.

Three-Time British Premier, **STANLEY BALDWIN**, Dies At 80.

The Throne Of Denmark Is Passed On To Frederick IX When His Beloved Father, **CHRISTIAN X**, Held Prisoner During The Nazi Occupation, Passes On At 77.

Paul Becomes King Of Greece On The Death Of His Brother **GEORGE II**.

PEOPLE

TIME MAN OF THE YEAR
GENERAL GEORGE C. MARSHALL

Appointed Secretary of State earlier in the year, the former Army Chief of Staff and chief architect of the defeat of Germany and Japan develops a plan for the economic recovery of Europe with the United States providing the financial support. In his historic speech at Harvard University, he warns that Europe "must have substantial additional help or face economic, social and political deterioration of a very grave character."

A special committee appointed by Secretary Marshall concluded that not only would his plan stimulate the economies of France and Germany, but would prevent France from falling under the influence of the Communists.

HOWARD HUGHES TESTIFIES

The hearing room is jammed with reporters and spectators to hear Mr. Hughes who states that Senator Brewster, Committee Chairman, has offered to kill the inquiry into military aviation contracts if Hughes will agree to merge Pan-American Airlines with TWA.

Howard Hughes enters the hearing room of the Senate Investigating Committee.

Mr. Hughes raises his right hand to be sworn in.

Angry Hughes demands to be allowed to cross-question Senator Brewster who he accuses of telling a pack of lies about him, blemishing his reputation.

WHAT A YEAR IT WAS!

Eisenhower Appointed President Of Columbia University.

IN A BREAK FROM ITS TRADITION, OXFORD AWARDS GEORGE MARSHALL HONORARY DEGREE.

TY COBB

Jailed For Being Drunk On A Public Highway After Snide Remarks To A Local Justice Of The Peace Who Nabbed Cobb's Girlfriend On A Traffic Violation.

Yeah, but you're ugly–and in the morning I'll be sober, but you'll still be ugly.

YOU'RE DRUNK!

Margaret Truman Makes Professional Radio Debut Singing With The Detroit Symphony.

Margaret Truman Is Guest Soprano At The Hollywood Bowl.

The Richest Blond In The World, Doris Duke Cromwell, Hired By Harper's Bazaar To Work In Its Paris Bureau.

On Her Arrival In Spain, Argentina's **Eva Peron** Is Greeted With A 21-Gun Salute.

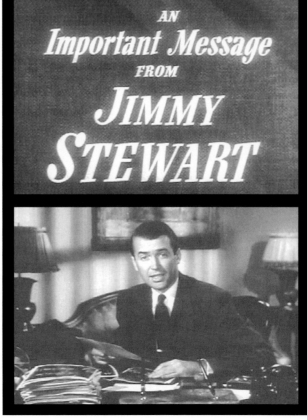

AN Important Message FROM JIMMY STEWART

Holding pictures of starving people all over the world, Jimmy Stewart appeals to Americans to send contributions and cut down on wheat and meat consumption so we can "Save The Peace."

1947 ADVERTISEMENT

How Good Is Your Taste?

a   b   c   d

Same lucky people in each photograph! Yet only one of these pictures merits a place of honor in your album. That's what the experts tell us. So, look them over. Let your own good taste be your guide. And then, just to be certain that you agree with the experts, read the answer in the upside down print right next door.

Of course, you picked the winner! Photograph "C" wins hands down! Now, let's look at the others. The background of "A" is too confused. "D" is as worn-out and tired as a Joe Miller joke. Just look at those feet and legs in "B." Our inspiration is "How Good Is Your Taste?", by Sanford E. Gerard, Doubleday, $3.00.

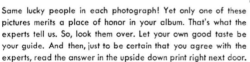

Packed with Good Taste!

Right The First Time!

● And with good taste as your guide, you can easily spot the winner in chewing gum! It's the sophisticated choice—*deliciously different* Teaberry Gum. For that mountain-grown teaberry flavor is refreshingly cool . . . juicy . . . exhilarating! And like other discriminating people, you'll prize the smoother, finer quality of the gum itself. So, *today* discover the thrill of Teaberry Gum . . . and you'll prefer it always!

CLARK'S TEABERRY GUM

Carry It with You Always

Product of Clark Bros. Chewing Gum Company of Pittsburgh, Penna., © 1947 C.B.C.G. Co.

COUPLING

- ♥ Diana Barrymore & John Howard
- ♥ Mary Spencer Churchill & Captain Christopher Soames
- ♥ Colleen Dewhurst & James Vickery
- ♥ Ann Dvorak & Igor De Navrotsky
- ♥ Dale Evans & Roy Rogers
- ♥ Ella Fitzgerald & Ray Brown
- ♥ Sterling Hayden & Betty Ann de Noon
- ♥ Jascha Heifetz & Frances Spiegelberg
- ♥ Dean Jagger & Gloria Ling
- ♥ Van Johnson & Eve Abbott Wynn
- ♥ Johnny Johnston & Kathryn Grayson
- ♥ Henry Luce III & Patricia Livingston Potter
- ♥ Virginia Mayo & Michael O'Shea
- ♥ Carmen Miranda & David Sebastian
- ♥ William S. Paley & Barbara Cushing Mortimer
- ♥ Sam Peckinpah & Marie Selland
- ♥ Anthony Quayle & Dorothy Hyson

Separate Tables & Beds

Tommy Dorsey Separates From His Second Wife, Pat.

UNCOUPLING

Oleg Cassini & Gene Tierney

Doris Day & George Weidler

Ava Gardner & Artie Shaw

Greer Garson & Richard Ney

James Hilton & Galina Kopineck Hilton

Hedy Lamarr & John Loder

Eugene Ormandy & Steffy Goldner Ormandy

Sylvia Sidney & Luther Adler

Jan Sterling & Jack Merivale

Dorothy Parker & Alan Campbell

Orson Welles & Rita Hayworth

Gig Young & Sheila Stapler

1947

Baltimore Judge E. Paul Mason Upholds The State's Ban On **"The Outlaw"** Starring **Jane Russell** Because Of The Exposure Of Her Large Breasts.

SHE REALLY TRIPPED UP

Joan Crawford, *Who Broke Her Right Ankle Three Times, Trips On A Rug In Her House And Falls Down The Stairs Tearing A Ligament In Her Left Ankle.*

SMOKEY THE MINK

Veronica Lake Put Out Fire On Her Husband's Plane By Smothering It With Her Mink Coat.

Devoted Giants' Fan Tallulah Bankhead Refers To The New York Yankees As Cold And Colorless Perfectionists Who Bore The Bloomers Off Of Her.

HELEN HAYES
Gets Ten Stitches In Her Arm After Slipping In The Shower.

MARY PICKFORD Is Sued By Director Gregory LaCava For Breach Of An Oral Contract To Film "One Touch Of Venus."

Yachtsman Errol Flynn Makes A Farewell Address To Hollywood From Kingston, Jamaica.

Babe Ruth Discharged From Manhattan Hospital Three Months After Surgery On His Neck.

IT AIN'T MUCH, BUT IT'S HOME
Princess Elizabeth and Philip Mountbatten were given a place of their own by her father – a vine-covered country home in Sunninghill Park set on 300 acres and just a few moats away from Windsor Castle.

WHAT A YEAR IT WAS!

Births Are At All-Time High In New York City With 170,469 Recorded For This Year.

NEW YORK

Total Deaths: 80,733

General Dwight D. Eisenhower Muses That He Would Like To Be Remembered As The Chief Of Staff Who Did Something About The Army's Cooking.

American Opera Singer And Film Star, Grace Moore, Killed In Airplane Crash Shortly After Take-Off In Copenhagen Along With 20 Others Including Prince Gustaf Adolf, Eldest Son Of The Crown Prince Of Sweden.

ELEANOR ROOSEVELT ACCEPTS MILITARY DECORATION AWARDED POSTHUMOUSLY TO HER LATE HUSBAND.

PASSINGS:

Notorious **Gangster Al "Scarface" Capone** Dies At 48 Of Syphilis After An "Illustrious" Career Which Included Control Of The Chicago Underworld In The 1920's And The Notorious Prohibition Bootleg Wars During Which He Ordered Over 300 Gangland Slayings.

Benjamin "Bugsy" Siegel Victim Of Gangland Execution Dead At 41.

Ogden Mills Reid, Editor Of New York Herald Tribune Dies At 65.

Carrie Chapman Catt, American Suffrage Activist And Founder Of League Of Women Voters Dies At 88.

Evalyn Walsh McLean, Owner Of The Hope Diamond, Dies At 60 After A Life Of Extreme Gaiety And Intense Tragedy.

British Philosopher, **Alfred North Whitehead**, Mathematician And Philosopher Who Collaborated With Bertrand Russell, Dies At 86.

New York's "Little Flower," Former Mayor **Fiorello La Guardia** Dies At 65.

You go, weather or no, *on the Water Level Route*

It's Always Fair Weather for travel aboard New York Central's *Great Steel Fleet*. From the cozy vantage point of your Club Car easy chair, it matters neither to your plans nor your peace of mind when sleet glazes the highways or clouds blot out the winter sky.

© 1947, New York Central Railroad Company

NEW
Streamliners and Dreamliners

This year, a vast new fleet of daylight streamliners and overnight, all-room Dreamliners will spotlight the NEW in New York Central.

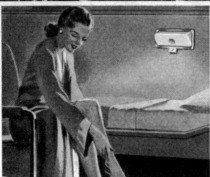

Rest Assured! A deep-mattressed bed, cradled by the smooth Water Level Route, invites you to rest . . . and you rest assured that Central's dependable all-weather transportation will get you there tomorrow . . . refreshed and ready for the day ahead.

Deep Seated Comfort. The comfort of a thrifty reclining seat in one of Central's de luxe, air-conditioned coaches goes deeper than feather-soft cushions or stabilized car springs. For there's the deep down *mental* comfort of traveling in the world's safest way!

NEW YORK CENTRAL
The Water Level Route—You Can Sleep

NEW YORK CENTRAL SYSTEM

40

Girls strut their stuff for the Miss Brevity Contest at the Deauville Hotel in Miami.

HUMAN INTEREST

And the winner is Shirley Modell, pictured with the first runner-up.

MUSCLES GALORE

Musclemen from all over Canada converge on Montreal to compete in flexing their muscles.

And here's a close-up of the beaming **Miss Brevity**.

And here he is, flexing the best muscles of all – **Mr. Montreal**.

Boys Day Out At The Beauty Shop

This
Beauty Shop

OPEN TODAY
for
MEN PATRONS ONLY

ABA

Pals Zeke Manners, Peter Lynn Hayes and Art Linkletter decide to luxuriate at the local beauty shop.

Getting ready for their beauty treatment, the boys put on capes.

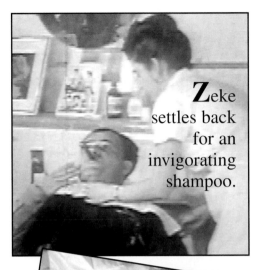

Zeke settles back for an invigorating shampoo.

Peter Lynn Hayes plays the big bad wolf as he's about to lay back in the shampoo chair.

Getting the full treatment, Peter takes one more bite of his fingernails.

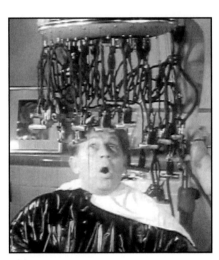

Art Linkletter decides to have a permanent but is overwhelmed by the equipment – He can't see the forest for the tresses.

Settling under the hair dryers, these guys can dish the dirt with the best of the girls.

"Well, I wouldn't want this repeated, but did you hear about..."

Four times in one night. Can you imagine?

Mummer's Parade Ushers In The New Year

24 competing clubs spare neither pains nor expense to produce gorgeous exhibits, many costing up to $25,000.

They march gaily in sub-freezing temperatures during the winter's worst storm which blanketed the entire East Coast.

A driving snowstorm fails to deter Philadelphia's Mummers or fans from their 46th parade ushering in the New Year.

One of the favorite exhibits is a Dick Tracy shoot-out using two-way wrist radios.

Once again, the Mummers with their elaborate pageant bring a carefree New Year's to Philadelphia.

WHAT A YEAR IT WAS!

Wouldn't you like some candy?

If you were a weather forecaster and the rain and the shine had gone unscientific on you and fouled up your prophecies and you needed some brightening up, wouldn't *you* like some candy?

If you were a test pilot and you had spent the first half of the morning flirting with the speed of sound and now you needed some quick energy without spoiling your appetite for lunch, wouldn't *you* like some candy?

If you were a beauty operator and you'd snarled up your appointments and the customers were getting irritated and impatient, wouldn't it help to stop for a moment and ask each one, "Wouldn't you like some *candy?*"

If you were preparing the table for Thanksgiving dinner and you wanted to top off the feast with something delicious but not too filling, don't you think it would be nice to say, "Wouldn't you like some *candy?*"

Yes...Most everybody likes Candy!

IN BOX

IN BAR

IN BAG

CANDY IS DELICIOUS FOOD

Enjoy some every day!

COUNCIL ON CANDY of the NATIONAL CONFECTIONERS' ASSOCIATION...One North La Salle Street, Chicago 2, Illinois

© 1947—NCA ...an organization devoted to the dissemination of authoritative information about candy

45

1947

29-Year Old Oklahoma Faith Healer, Oral Roberts, Begins Broadcasting Over The Radio.

The United States Becomes The Only Superpower Without Peacetime Conscription As Military Draft Ends.

President Truman Grants Pardon To Over 1,000 Who Evaded World War II Draft.

52,000 March In American Legion Parade In New York.

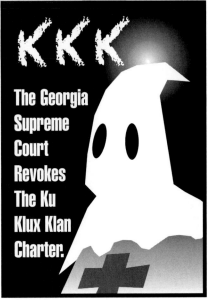

KKK

The Georgia Supreme Court Revokes The Ku Klux Klan Charter.

Civil War

THE LAST CIVIL WAR VETERAN DIES.

U.S. Army Air Force Celebrates Its 40th Anniversary.

U.S. AIR FORCE BECOMES INDEPENDENT OF ARMY.

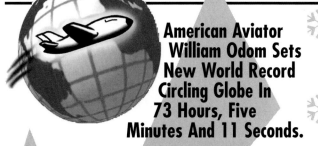

American Aviator William Odom Sets New World Record Circling Globe In 73 Hours, Five Minutes And 11 Seconds.

The Spruce Goose, World's Largest Airplane, Ascended 70 Feet Into The Air And Flew One Mile Piloted By Howard Hughes. Built By Mr. Hughes For The U.S. Government During The War At A Cost Of $25 Million (He Contributed $7 Million), The Project Is Under Investigation By A Congressional Committee.

The XC-99, The World's Largest Land Aircraft, Makes Its First Flight In San Diego. The Aircraft Has The Capability Of Carrying 400 Troops Or Cargo Weighing Up To 100,000 Pounds.

FASTER THAN A SPEEDING BULLET

After 24 Years, The U.S. Recaptures The World Record With Its Army Lockheed P-80R Shooting Star Jet Traveling At Speeds Of Up To 623.8 MPH.

Blizzard Blankets New York In 28 Inches Of Snow.

Britain Sees Its Worst Winter Since 1894.

150 Perish In Dance-Hall Fire In British Sector Of Berlin.

SYDNEY, AUSTRALIA IS BOMBARDED WITH HAIL STONES AS BIG AS CRICKET BALLS.

BABY IT'S COLD OUTSIDE

Record Cold Temperature Is Recorded In The Yukon At 83 Degrees Below Zero. Button Up That Overcoat!

UFO

Idaho Businessman Kenneth Arnold Sights Nine Saucerlike Objects Streaking Across The Cascade Range At "1,200 MPH In Formation, Like The Tail Of A Kite" As He Is Piloting His Plane To Portland. Discounting More Than 30 Other Ground Sightings In The U.S. And Canada, The Air Force Calls Them A "Prank Of Nature" And Psychiatrists Call Them Mass Hallucinations.

UFO

Flying Saucers Reported In The United States With Alleged Government Cover-Up Of A UFO Crash Near Roswell, New Mexico.

1947

Los Angeles Examiner

Assigns 12 Reporters To Cover The "Black Dahlia" Murder. Search For Killer Greatest Manhunt In Los Angeles History.

Manhattan Retires Last Trolley Car In Sentimental Ceremony.

Despite A Court Battle Waged By Its 300 Permanent Residents, The Historic Murray Hill Hotel Built In 1884 Falls Under The Wrecking Ball.

HOUSING

Six Million Families Move In With Friends And Relatives Because Of The Severe Housing Shortage.

First Mass-Produced Suburban Community Built In Levittown, New York On 1,200-Acre Long Island Potato Field With Houses Selling For $7,500.

Many College Graduates With Ph.D's Cannot Speak Or Write Correctly.

SEE SPOT R..U..N

Latest Statistics Show That Over Ten Million Adults Are Functionally Illiterate And Between 20% and 33% Of School Children Fail To Meet Their Grade's Reading Standards.

Bring On The Comic Books.

City College Of New York Celebrates Its 100th Anniversary.

What Are You, Some Kind Of Genius?

A Chicago Neurologist Lists Four Characteristics Of A Genius:

1. The Ability To Come Up With New Artistic, Literary, Scientific, Philosophic Or Practical Ideas

2. Complete Disinterest In Personal Gain

3. A Quality And Permanency In Work Achieved

4. World Recognition

WHAT A YEAR IT WAS!

Use on-the-spot storage space for pots and pans — 2 big storage drawers with finger-touch, roller-bearing action save steps, provide handy space for cooking utensils.

Look at the ample work space —fluorescent top lamp — Generous work space in center for making gravies, mixing, serving, etc., without reaching over hot burners. Beautiful chrome lamp (see below) lights the top surface. Convenient interval timer warns you when cooking's done.

WAKE UP THE NEIGHBORS, MRS. REVERE!

AND TELL THEM HOW YOU FOUND EVERYTHING YOU WANTED FOR A LOT LESS MONEY...

Tell them this new Kalamazoo is 40 inches wide—not the usual 36 or 38 inches. Tell them you discovered more cooking, more working space and a giant 18-inch oven that holds a 25-pound turkey.

Available now at your Kalamazoo dealer's or department store—check all 26 features ... then compare prices!

KALAMAZOO STOVE & FURNACE CO., 561 Rochester Ave., Kalamazoo 6, Mich.

the big KALAMAZOO gas range
with oversize 18-inch oven—not usual 16-inch

Measure this giant 18-inch oven — Bakes four 10-in. pies or 8 loaves of bread at once. Bakes cakes and rolls to a golden brown. Heavily insulated—fully porcelain enameled. Automatic precision oven regulator. Automatic oven light.

Boast about the "Flame Ray" broiler — 6 inches deep—generous room for steaks, chops, fish. Flame Ray principle applies heat scientifically for tender, juicy results. Non-spatter, non-smoke broiler grid and pan are removable, easy to clean.

Breeze through your cleaning. Uniflow top is a single piece of china-white porcelain enamel from top of splasher back to oven door. All rounded corners. Square grates and burner bowls slip right into dishpan.

Uses city or bottled gas — Engineered for the most efficient use of bottled gas —clean, controlled heat instantly. Also burns manufactured or natural gas. Have 100 different degrees of heat with these easy-cleaning thrift burners.

HOME APPLIANCES BY KALAMAZOO
QUALITY LEADERS SINCE 1901

49

Love And Marriage And All That Stuff

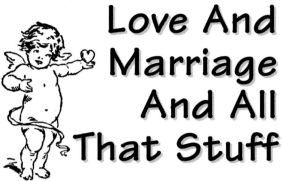

50% Of Men Who Marry Tie The Knot Before Age 25.

50% Of Women Who Marry Tie The Knot Before Age 22.

The Average American Woman Between 19 and 25 Receives Three Marriage Proposals.

The Favorite Site For A Marriage Proposal Is His Car, Followed By Her Home Or A Public Place.

One Or More Persons Live With Married Couples Throughout Their Married Life.

One Couple Out Of Five Moves In With Relatives.

On An Average, Pregnancy Occurs After The First Year Of Marriage With The Last Of Three Children Born By The Time The Woman Reaches Age 28.

Some Say I Do, Some Say I Don't Or Won't

An Increasing Number Of Men And Women Opt For Staying Single – The Women Because Of The Lack Of Eligible Men And The Men Just Because...

One In Seven Married Women Do Not Have Children.

There Is A 50-50 Chance A Couple Will Be Together For 39 Years.

Developing A Mutually-Satisfying Sex Life Takes The Biggest Adjustment And Most Amount Of Time.

Opposites Do Not Attract As Engaged Couples Show A Definite Preference For Similarities In Religious, Family Cultural Background And Interests.

What a _wonderful_ way to feed a baby!
CLAPP'S "MEAL-IN-A-DISH"

Come on, mothers! Here's a really great idea in baby feeding!

It's a _balanced_ combination of meat and garden vegetables—all in ONE dish! It's pressure-cooked and strained. A real "Meal-in-a-Dish" for your baby.

Take Clapp's Liver Soup as an example . . .

First, there's tender beef liver—chock-full of vitamins! There are tomatoes, carrots, potatoes, rice, barley, celery, and a hint of onion.

8 fine foods in a single dish!

That's just _one_ of Clapp's "Meal-in-a-Dish" treats for your baby. Clapp's makes _five_ different kinds . . .

1. Clapp's Vegetables-with-Liver (_Liver Soup_)
2. Clapp's Vegetables-with-Beef
3. Clapp's Vegetables-with-Lamb
4. Clapp's Vegetables-with-Bacon
5. Clapp's Vegetables-with-Chicken (_Chicken Soup_)

They're all wonderful in flavor, wonderful in nourishment . . . made as only Clapp's can make baby foods, as Clapp's has made baby foods for two generations of babies to thrive on!

Your grocer is featuring Clapp's "Meal-in-a-Dish" treats right now in Clapp's Strained Foods for little babies and Clapp's Junior Foods for toddlers. Get your baby a week's supply today.

Specially featured at your grocer's this month
BUY A WEEK'S SUPPLY TODAY!

PRODUCTS OF AMERICAN HOME FOODS.

Start your baby on
CLAPP'S BABY FOODS
the _first_ baby foods

CLAPP'S STRAINED FOODS ★ JUNIOR FOODS ★ BABY CEREALS

Women Lose Millions Of Jobs As Companies Hire Returning Veterans.

Over One Million Vets Enroll In Colleges under The "G.I. Bill Of Rights" Bringing Enrollment Up To 2.5 Million Students.

97% Of Male Veteran Heads Of Households Are Employed.

INSTRUMENTAL IN SECURING FULL MILITARY RANK FOR WOMEN, COLONEL FLORENCE BLANCHFIELD, SUPERINTENDENT OF ARMY NURSES, BECOMES FIRST WOMAN TO RECEIVE A COMMISSION IN THE U.S. ARMY.

U.S. Post Office Introduces The Air Letter, A Sheet Of Paper That Folds Into A Stamped Envelope.

Harry S. Truman Inaugurates Spare-One-Turkey On Thanksgiving Tradition.

WORLD WAR II STATISTICS

15% Of Americans Were In The Armed Forces

Cost Of The War: $340 Billion Dollars

U.S. Fatalities: 313,000

Missing In Action: 17,126

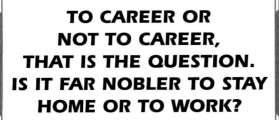

**TO CAREER OR
NOT TO CAREER,
THAT IS THE QUESTION.
IS IT FAR NOBLER TO STAY
HOME OR TO WORK?**

A Housewife Speaks

A CAREER WIFE SPEAKS

66 I'd feel trapped if I stayed home. My job keeps me mentally alert.

66 I'm highly educated and well-trained in what I do. It would be a waste to throw it all away as soon as I marry.

66 Working is more constructive than playing bridge or gossiping.

66 My additional income insures that our children get a good education and excellent medical care.

66 My husband and I have a better mutual understanding and we communicate as equals on financial matters.

66 Where would we be if Madame Curie stopped working as soon as she married? Women have great contributions to make outside of their homes.

66 Marriage and a career can work as one enhances the other and makes the time spent at home much more special.

*B*eing a housewife is a career and it takes a lot of hard work and concentration to make it successful.

*M*arriage and motherhood are the most important jobs a woman can have.

*B*eing a housewife is not all drudgery. A clever, creative wife can find ways of brightening her home and making it more livable.

*Y*oung children need a lot of affection and should not be turned over to a house-keeper.

A wife should show great interest in her husband's career and be sympathetic with the problems he faces. If she has a career too she will be more interested in her own problems than in his.

*I*f women were meant to have careers, they would not be capable of bearing children. Men should definitely wear the pants in the family.

*R*unning a successful home is a full-time job. A woman should not have too many outside interests so that she doesn't neglect her wifely duties thereby putting the marriage in jeopardy.

AND THESE ARE HIS GOOD QUALITIES

In Kansas City A Woman Sues For Divorce On The Grounds That Her Husband Is Disagreeable, Morbid, Cool, Bitter, Jealous, Headstrong, Picayunish, Loathsome, Insulting, Miserly, Gluttonish, Temperamental, Contemptuous, Inattentive, Uncivil And Inconsiderate.

What's for dinner, Duchess?

Prediction: The new wives of 1947 are going to have more fun in the kitchen.

Previous cooking experience is desirable, perhaps, but not essential. There are so many new easy-to-use foods, so many new ways to prepare foods, so many interesting ways to serve foods, cooking will be a novel and exciting adventure.

Further prediction: Cheese dishes will be featured more often on their menus. They'll know that cheese gives tastiness and variety to meals. And cheese, like milk (nature's most nearly perfect food), is rich in protein, calcium, phosphorus, in vitamins A and G.

Yes, we have a personal interest in cheese. For Kraft, pioneer in cheese, is a unit of National Dairy. And what we've said about housewives using more cheese is entirely true.

It's also true that they're learning more about the whys and wherefores of food each year — just as the scientists in our laboratories are learning more about better ways to process, improve and supply it.

These men are backed by the resources of a great organization. They explore every field of dairy products, discover new ones. And the health of America benefits constantly by this National Dairy research.

Dedicated to the wider use and better understanding of dairy products as human food . . . as a base for the development of new products and materials . . . as a source of health and enduring progress on the farms and in the towns and cities of America.

NATIONAL DAIRY
PRODUCTS CORPORATION
AND AFFILIATED COMPANIES

The Times
They Are A Changin'

❏ **The Doctor Has Replaced The Banker As The Most Prestigious Profession, The Banker Now Sharing Second Place With Lawyers.**

❏ **A Film Of Dust On A Light Bulb May Absorb 20% Of The Light.**

❏ **A Pair Of The Tiniest Owls On Earth Called Elf Owls Are Discovered In The Joshua Tree National Monument In California.**

❏ **Glareless Glass Used For Military Field Glasses During The War Now Used On Television Monitors For Clearer, Sharper Pictures.**

❏ **Landlords And Tenants In Disputes Over Permission To Install Antennas On Roofs.**

Argentina Grants Vote To Women

The Serenity Prayer Becomes Part Of Alcoholics Anonymous Meetings.

NO JOKING MATTER

Milton Caniff's STEVE CANYON Comic Strip Debuts.

SUNNY, AMERICA'S SWEETHEART, Published By Fox Features, Is America's First Confession Comic Book With A Romance Theme.

$500,000 Donated By Thomas Lamont To Canterbury Cathedral For Restoration.

Search For A United Nations Site Ends On Presentation Of A Check For $8.5 Million Dollars By John D. Rockefeller III To Secretary-General Trygve Lie For The Purchase Of Property Bordering New York's East River.

Bedouin Shepherd Boy Discovers Leather Scrolls In Dead Sea Cave Containing Copy Of Old Testament Dating From 1st Century B.C.

THAT'S A LOT OF COOKIES
Girl Scouts From 22 Countries Visit The United Nations.

WHAT A YEAR IT WAS!

55

MISS AMERICA
Barbara Walker
Memphis,
Tennessee

The Apple Pan Opens Its Doors In Los Angeles And Begins Serving The Best Hamburgers In Town.

NEW YORK TRANSIT DOUBLES FARES TO

$.10

FIRST INCREASE SINCE 1904

GREYHOUND EQUIPS ITS BUSES WITH TWO-WAY RADIOS.

I WON'T DANCE, DON'T ASK ME

200 Arthur Murray Dancers Win Strike For Collective Bargaining.

Going Price Of Black-Market Baby Set At $2,500.

Birthrate: 2.8 Per Family

Native-Born Americans Tend To Be Taller Than Their Immigrant Counterparts.

The Birth Rate Is Higher On Farms Than In Cities.

WHEN GOOD PEOPLE DO BAD THINGS

The Chicago Crime Commission Reveals The Following Reasons Why Honest People Commit Embezzlement:
- *Pressure Of Keeping Up With The Joneses*
- *Medical Emergency*
- *Having A Mistress*
- *Low Salary*

Area Codes Are Devised To Meet Post-World War II Demand For Telephone Service.

1947

Everglades National Park Established As A Refuge For Endangered Species Of Animals And Plants By Act Of Congress.

A New Ordinance Is Passed In Hempstead, New York Requiring Horses To Be Equipped With Head And Tail Lights After Dark.

FAMINE SWEEPS RUMANIA ENDANGERING THOUSANDS.

Eisenhower Launches Drive To Raise $170 Million To Aid European Jews.

Truman Urges Americans To Participate In March Of Dimes Charity Drive.

American People Asked By President Truman To Reduce Meat And Poultry Consumption To Make More Food Available For Famine-Struck Europe.

270-Car Friendship Train Arrives In New York With Food And Supplies For European Relief.

London Imposes Restrictions On Food, Petrol And Travel.

SOMETHING TO CROW ABOUT

According To Harvard Professor Alfred S. Romer, The Egg Did Come Before The Chicken.

Now, Why Did The Chicken Cross The Road???

Truman Seeks Mandatory Military Training In U.S.

WHAT A YEAR IT WAS!

NEW WORDS &

A.E.C.
United States Atomic Energy Commission

Air Letter
A Single Sheet Pre-Stamped Letter Which Folds Into Its Own Envelope.

Astra Dome
Observation Deck Built On Some Of The Cars Of The General Motors "Train Of Tomorrow."

Atomic Itch
Skin Irritation And High Fever Caused By Exposure To Atomic Radiation.

Baby Sit
To Take Care Of A Baby While The Parents Are Out.

Bathyscaphe
A Device Allowing Dissension Into The Ocean.

Blackmarketing
Operating On The Black Market.

Chain Reaction
A Series Of Results, One Caused By Another.

Dollar Crisis
Imbalance Of Trade.

Civilian
A Temporary Member Of A Group.

Electronarcosis
A Mild Electric Shock To The Brain Used In The Treatment Of The Mentally Ill.

ERP
European Recovery Plan.

Flying Saucer
A Mysterious Object Flying At Great Heights And High Speeds Sighted Over Oregon And Other Parts Of The Country.

Freedom Train
A Train Traveling Through The U.S. Housing An Exhibit Of Important Historical Documents.

Friendship Train
A Train Traveling From Los Angeles To New York Collecting Contributions Of Food For Europe.

EXPRESSIONS

Hurricane-Hunter Plane
A Plane For Searching Out And Locating Hurricanes.

Police State
A State Controlled By The Government.

Marshall Plan
Secretary Of State George C. Marshall's Plan For Financial Aid To Western Europe To Assist In A Long-Term Plan For Recovery And Restoration.

Trumanburger
A Sandwich Consisting Of Mashed Beans And Barbecue Sauce.

New Look
An Innovative New Style For Women's Clothing Introduced By Christian Dior.

Truman Doctrine
President Harry S. Truman's Policy For Giving Financial Aid To Nations For Rehabilitation And Resistance To Communism.

Ultrafax High-Speed
Communication System Utilizing Television.

Watchdog Commission
Government Commission Set Up To Observe Trouble Spot.

Phone Vision
A Principle Developed By Zenith Radio Corporation For Transmitting Television Over Phone Wires

1947 ADVERTISEMENT

WHO gets HOW MUCH
of the
RAILROAD DOLLAR?

(A REPORT TO THE PEOPLE FOR 1946)

You, and all Americans, look to the railroads not only to *take* you places, but also to *bring* you things —food, clothing, fuel, and just about everything else you use in your home and in your business. For rendering this dependable service to 140 million people, and for hauling the heaviest peacetime traffic on record, the railroads received about 8 billion dollars in 1946. Let's see *who* got *how much* of each dollar paid the railroads.

FOR EMPLOYEES... 51.5¢

More than half of every dollar went to railroad employees in wages and salaries.

33¢ FOR MATERIALS

Much of this 33¢ the railroads spent for materials, fuel and other supplies was, in turn, spent by the *railroad suppliers* to pay *their* employees. So, directly or indirectly, by far the largest part of the railroad dollar goes to pay wages.

6.2¢ FOR TAXES

This part of the railroad dollar went to Federal, state, and local governments to be used—the same as your own taxes—to help maintain schools, courts, roads, police and fire protection, and for various other public services and institutions. None of this tax money is spent on railroad tracks or terminals.

FOR INSURANCE POLICY-HOLDERS, INVESTORS IN BONDS, AND FOR RENTS . . .

6.6¢

Most of this 6.6¢ was paid to those people who lend money to the railroads — including those millions of thrifty Americans who invest indirectly in the railroads through their insurance policies and savings accounts. The average rate of interest which railroads pay on their bonds and other obligations is less than 4 per cent.

2.7¢ FOR IMPROVEMENTS AND OWNERS

And so after they had paid for wages, materials, taxes, and necessary charges upon their obligations, the railroads had only 2.7¢ left out of each dollar they took in in 1946. Out of this 2.7¢ they must pay for the improvements necessary to keep railroad property abreast of public needs, before anything is available for dividends to their owners.

ASSOCIATION OF **AMERICAN RAILROADS** WASHINGTON 6, D. C.

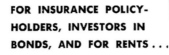

IN PARTNERSHIP WITH ALL AMERICA

BUSINESS

★ WORLD BANK OPENS GRANTING FRANCE $250 MILLION AND HOLLAND $195 MILLION IN RECONSTRUCTION LOANS.

★ FORD MOTORS CREATES THE FIRST PENSION PLAN FOR THE AUTOMOBILE INDUSTRY. AVERAGE WORKER WILL RECEIVE $77 MONTHLY ON RETIREMENT.

★ U.S. STEEL DEMANDS OPEN SHOP FOR 1947 WAGE CONTRACT.

★ REGAL DRUGSTORE CHAIN FOUNDED BY BERNARD SHULMAN.

★ THE UNITED NATION'S INTERNATIONAL MONETARY FUND BEGINS DOING BUSINESS.

★ 35,000 MINERS GO OUT AS JOHN L. LEWIS CALLS STRIKE FOR MINERS KILLED IN CENTRALIA EXPLOSION.

3-M Introduces First Magnetic Recording Tape For Commercial Purposes

PAN AMERICAN OFFERS FLIGHT AROUND THE WORLD FOR $1,700

1947 ADVERTISEMENT

JULY
Mobil-Care

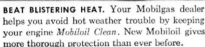
Mobil Crankcase Check-up

BEAT BLISTERING HEAT. Your Mobilgas dealer helps you avoid hot weather trouble by keeping your engine *Mobiloil Clean.* New Mobiloil gives more thorough protection than ever before.

NEW MOBILOIL helps keep engine parts—pistons, rings and valves—fully lubricated . . . and free of deposits that waste fuel, oil, power. There's less risk of costly repairs.

EXPERTS WHO KNOW YOUR CAR protect all chassis friction points with Summer Mobilgreases, following a scientific Mobilubrication chart of your make and model car. At the same time, your Mobilgas dealer looks for hidden dangers!

PREVENT ROAD TROUBLE. He checks fan belt for wear—inspects oil filter, air cleaner, spark plugs, windshield wipers, other vital parts to make sure they're working right, won't cause trouble!

Mobilubrication and Complete Car Inspection

Mobilgas · Mobiloil

62

SUN'S FUN FOR YOU...
BUT PROTECT THAT CAR!

For Power Spurts when you need them...

Flying Horsepower from
Mobilgas Special

Enjoy fast getaway in traffic!...extra pep for passing, hills, the open road!...try Flying Horsepower from Mobilgas Special, America's Favorite Premium Gasoline!

Mobil-Care means better Car-Care
See Your
Mobilgas Dealer

Mobilgas
SOCONY-VACUUM

AT THE SIGN OF FRIENDLY SERVICE
SOCONY-VACUUM OIL CO., INC. and Affiliates: Magnolia Petroleum Co., General Petroleum Corp.

Mobil Tires—Expert Service

NOW—FOR YOUR SAFETY your Mobilgas dealer carries dependable, long-mileage Mobil Tires, guaranteed by the makers of Mobilgas and Mobiloil.

THE MOBIL TIRE has been proved in millions of miles of use—never has a tire made so many friends—so fast! You get the tire quality you want—the service you want!

• Mobilubrication •

As the world observes the 100th anniversary of the birth of Thomas A. Edison, Dr. Charles F. Ketterling notes: *"As truly as though each of us had been named in his last will and testament, every industry, business, profession and home using electricity is a beneficiary of the labors of this great man."*

BUSINESS TIPS ON HOW TO GET AHEAD IN BUSINESS FROM SOME OF AMERICA'S LEADING INDUSTRIALISTS

1. Make Sure The Boss Sees Your Work So That You Can Get Recognition.

2. Create Your Own Opportunities As Luck Plays A Very Small Part In Achieving Success.

3. Don't Buy A House As It Could Keep You From A Better Opportunity.

4. If Your Boss Doesn't Approve Of The Job You're Doing, Quit.

5. Always Try To Work With Someone Who Knows More Than You.

6. Concentrate On Achieving Your Own Success And Don't Worry About Other People Around You Becoming Successful.

7. Be Self-Disciplined.

8. Don't Watch The Clock— Just Get The Job Done.

9. Don't Worry About The Past—Concentrate On Today.

10. Believe That There Is A Solution To Every Problem.

WHAT A YEAR IT WAS!

Now your gift of a Kodak camera will capture
MORE CHRISTMAS

With Kodacolor Film and blue flash lamps, it's easy to get— even with a Brownie.

"Takes a lot of doing?" No, just a Kodak camera with flash, and Kodak Verichrome Film.

For the full color of Christmas outdoors, Kodacolor Film makes all the difference.

All of the cameras shown here take both black-and-white and full-color pictures...day or night

Kodak Reflex Camera, $120

Price includes Field Case . . . Flasholder extra. For the reflex-camera "fan" who appreciates these superior features—twin *f*/3.5 lenses, both *Lumenized* . . . Flash Koda-matic Shutter, 7 speeds to 1/200 . . . rigid cast-aluminum body. A superb camera for color, flash—all modern picture making.

(Prices do not include tax)

Brownie Cameras, $2.75 to $9

Illustrated: Brownie Flash Six-20, $9. Flasholder extra.

A Brownie is always a *buy*. For a child or beginner. For anybody who wants to get good snapshots the easiest way. The Brownie Flash Six-20 gets them day or night . . . and, with Kodacolor Film, in full color.

Kodak Folding Cameras, $17.50 to $75

Kodak Monitors, $60 and $75; Kodak Vigilant Junior (without flash synchronization), $17.50.

Illustrated: Kodak Vigilant *f*/4.5, $53. Flasholder extra.

These famous favorites, providing 2¼ x 3¼ negatives in a camera that is compact, easy-to-carry, now make full-color snapshots (with Koda-color Film) as well as black-and-white, and most of them may be equipped with flash for night shots.

"Kodak" is a trade mark

Kodak Miniature Cameras, $50 to $75

Kodak Flash Bantam *f*/4.5, $50   Kodak 35 *f*/4.5, $50

Illustrated: Kodak 35 *f*/3.5, with range finder, $75. Flasholder extra.

For your "Miniature" fan who wants crisp negatives for enlargements, and, with Kodachrome Film, slides in full color for projection or full-color prints.

Kodak is making more cameras than ever before, but the demand is greater, too. Consult your dealer.
EASTMAN KODAK CO.
Rochester 4, N. Y.

Kodak

This is the warehouse of the Bubble Gum King in McAllen, Texas.

The sole importer of this fascinating commodity made from latex in Mexican factories is Andrew J. Paris, shown above testing the bubble capacity of a piece of gum.

Paris gives out samples at a local schoolhouse and the kids do a little Bubble, Bubble, Toil and Trouble.

BUBBLE GUM KING

His office staff knows the rules of the game and are experts in the inflationary art.

1947 ADVERTISEMENT

First thing in the morning . . .   *when everybody's rushed . . .*   *and tastes are fussy . . .*

Try Borden's – the new instant coffee made especially for breakfast!

We don't have to tell *you* folks how nice it would be to have *instant* coffee for breakfast — for that early morning rush, when time's so short.

"Sure," you say, "but *how good is the coffee?* Show us an instant coffee as swell as our best ground coffee — and we'll buy and bless you."

"Fair enough," says Borden. "We'll waste no words. Either Borden's has it, or you don't pay!

It'll taste as good as your favorite ground coffee every day — or your money back!"*

You see, Borden's was *made* for breakfast — not just for occasional use. It's all coffee — not a half-and-half café-type mixture! And what coffee! Serve it by the cup or by the pot. Serve it to the whole family. Serve it for every meal. If we aren't right, the treat's on us!

Tastes as good as your favorite ground coffee – or money back!

© THE BORDEN CO.

*Use at least half a jar of Borden's. Then, if you don't agree it tastes as good as your favorite ground coffee, send us the jar with the unused contents, and we'll cheerfully refund your money. The Borden Co., 350 Madison Ave., New York 17, N. Y.

this was the price that was

Bathing Cap	$	1.25
Billfold, Ladies		3.50
Billfold		2.75
Blankets		7.95
Christmas Tree Lamps		.10
Cigars (Box of 25)		3.75-8.75
Cigars		.15-.35

Record	$	1.25
Baseball		2.35
Bath Towel		.62
Coca-Cola		.05
Iron, electric		5.45
Flashlight Battery		.09
Wedding Ring, men's		8.50
Violin, student		9.95

GROCERIES

Apples (lb.)	$ .13
Beans, Navy (lb.)	.22
Beef Rib Roast (lb.)	.61
Bread, white (lb.)	.14
Butter (lb.)	.81
Cheese (lb.)	.64
Chicken (lb.)	.55
Coffee (lb.)	.47
Cornmeal (lb.)	.10
Eggs (doz.)	.76
Flour, wheat (lb.)	.10
Lard (lb.)	.33
Milk (qt.)	.21
Molasses, canned (18 oz.)	.16
Pork Chops (lb.)	.73
Bacon (lb.)	.80

Potatoes, Irish (15 lb.)	.77
Prunes, dried (lb.)	.25
Rice (lb.)	.19
Sugar (lb.)	.10
Veal, dried (lb.)	.90

Cameras

Kodak Brownie	$ 2.75-9.00
Kodak Folding	17.50-75.00
Kodak Miniature	50.00-75.00
Kodak Reflex	120.00

Ladies'
• CLOTHING •

LINGERIE

ITEM	PRICE
Bra	$7.50+
Girdle	7.50+
Slip (full)	3.50–6.00
Nylons	1.35

Thank You

La Shop

Blouse	$ 3.00
Cotton blouse	4.00
Dress (house)	2.95–4.00
Sweater	8.95–10.95
Swimsuit	7.95
Wool slacks	12.00

Average Salaries

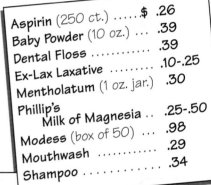

Average Income	$ 2,657.00 yr
Gas & Electricity Employee	2,994.00 yr
Medical/Health Services Employee	1,821.00 yr
Motion Picture Services	3,031.00 yr
Public School Teachers	2,261.00 yr
Radio Broadcasting & Television Employee	4,073.00 yr
Telephone Employee	2,583.00 yr

Aspirin (250 ct.)	$ .26
Baby Powder (10 oz.)	.39
Dental Floss	.39
Ex-Lax Laxative	.10–.25
Mentholatum (1 oz. jar.)	.30
Phillip's Milk of Magnesia	.25–.50
Modess (box of 50)	.98
Mouthwash	.29
Shampoo	.34

Pens (14-k gold filled)	$ 7.95
Pens	3.95
Razor sets	.49–3.79
Shaving Blades (pk. 12)	.25
Shaving Mug & Lotion	2.00
Muslin Sheets (2)	8.00
Muslin Pillowcases (2)	1.80
Silverware (6-pc.)	23.00
Thermometer	.74
Toaster (auto pop-up)	18.75

Hairbrush	$ 5.00–7.00
Lipstick.	1.00
Lipstick brush	1.00
Make-up cake	1.50
Make-up (Deluxe set).	10.75
Nail polish	.39
Nail polish sheen	.60
Ladies Perfume L'aimant & Emeraude	6.50

for THE PARTICULAR man

MEN'S CLOTHING

Cuff links (pair)	$ 7.95
Collar clip	1.50
Hat	4.00
Slacks (gabardine)	12.50–18.50
Sport coat	35.00–45.00
Suit (tropical worsted)	37.50
Tie	1.00
Shirt (white)	2.00
Sweater	8.95–13.95

Cough Drops	$ .05
Electric Clock	4.95–7.95
House Paint (gal.)	3.49
Tobacco Pouch lamb skin	2.50
Toothbrush	.50
Home Permanent	1.25
Toothpaste	.50
Washing Machine	229.00
Windshield Washers	6.25

DIAMONDS

1/4 CARAT	$ 95.00-210.00
1/2 CARAT	230.00-500.00
1 CARAT	600.00-1,165.00
2 CARAT	1,400.00-2,900.00

AUTOMOBILE DESIGNS

TRIUMPH Roadster epitomizes the small, popular English sport car, well-suited to the narrow, winding English roads, racy and lively in appearance. It seats three in front, has an old-fashioned rumble seat and a folding windshield for rumble passengers. Engine develops 16 European hp (65 U.S. hp.) The price in the U.S.: $4,150.

DELAGE Victoria has a raspberry-red body built by Figoni and Falaschi, famed European custom body makers, and a six-cylinder motor. Its natural leather seats hold four passengers. **Price: $15,000.**

ROLLS-ROYCE is the conservative, elder statesman of British motoring. Its radiator silhouette has changed only slightly since the first Rolls appeared in 1904. Because of superb workmanship, it is commonplace to find Rolls-Royces operating after 30 years' service. They cost from $18,450 to $19,200, are owned by kings and rajas.

LINCOLN CONTINENTAL by Ford has low, clean silhouette, firmly drawn fenders and functional, compact rear deck. The late Edsel Ford helped to design it. Despite its rather excessive grille, many designers regard it as the most beautiful U.S. car. The convertible model seats six, has a 120 hp V-12 motor, **costs $4,900.**

STUDEBAKER carries on a postwar trend toward blending fenders into the body and affords ample rear vision with big windows. Coupe seats five, has luggage space, **costs $1,942.**

HUDSON achieves low center of gravity by making the body and frame one unit so passengers sit between wheels. **Price: about $2,000.**

PASSINGS

HENRY FORD, inventor of the Model T and Model A Fords, and father of modern mass production methods, dies at 84 leaving a fortune estimated at $625 million.

French car manufacturer **ETTORE BUGATTI** dies at 66.

WILLIAM DURANT, founder of General Motors in 1908, dies at 86.

WHAT A YEAR IT WAS!

1947 ADVERTISEMENT

To my Darling

I tried to think of something that would be as gay and dashing and wonderful as you are.

So, my Darling, it's a Nash—all for you. A beautiful new Nash "600," to be exact.

I'm sorry about that mud on the wheels—but I'm human—I had to sneak it out for a whirl last night.

Your new Nash is the sweetest-running car I ever had my hands on. It rides like sheer velvet.

Handles like a dream. We went sailing over Schoolhouse Hill as if it didn't exist at all.

I don't want to spoil your fun, but don't miss that little button on the dash called the Weather Eye. It keeps the air always fresh, clean and heated to perfection. You don't even need a coat!

I admit it looks extravagant. But it's a Nash …and you'll be enjoying it 'til the kids grow up.

Merry Christmas, Darling.

You'll be Ahead with **Nash** *Great Cars Since 1902*

Nash Motors Division, Nash-Kelvinator Corporation, Detroit

Under The Leadership Of Justin Dart, United Drugs, A Boston-Based Company, Is Renamed Rexall Drug.

Calgary Becomes Administrative Center Of Exploration And Development After Oil Discovery At Leduc.

Galvin Manufacturing Renamed Motorola, After Its Car Radios.

Thread Mills Changes Its Name To Fieldcrest Mills To Promote Brand Identification.

First Nationwide Phone Strike Hits U.S. As 350,000 Workers Walk Off The Job.

TIME CLOCK

• **U.S.** Steel And Union Agree On 15-Cent Hourly Pay Raise.

• **T**he Controversial Taft-Hartley Labor Bill Aimed At Restraining Union Power Becomes Law Despite President Truman's Veto Who Proclaims That It "Contains The Seeds Of Discord Which Will Plague This Nation."

• **T**ruman Asks Congress For Wage And Price Controls.

• **W**illiam Green Elected President Of A.F.L.

• **J**ohn L. Lewis Takes U.A.W. Out Of A.F.L.

BASKIN-ROBBINS IS CREATED THROUGH THE MERGER OF TWO SMALL CHAINS IN SOUTHERN CALIFORNIA OWNED SEPARATELY BY BROTHERS-IN-LAW BURTON "BUTCH" BASKIN AND IRVINE ROBBINS.

●

CO-FOUNDER OF DREYER'S, JOSEPH EDY, LEAVES COMPANY.

ICE CREAM ON A STICK MACHINE ACCELERATES PRODUCTION
Los Angeles Based Creameries Of America, Inc. Installs New Machines Called Vita-Freeze Which Automatically Chocolate Dips A Square Of Ice-Cream, Inserts A Stick And Packages All In One Quick Operation.

Atlantic Records Incorporates.

Howard Hughes' TWA Moves Its Headquarters To New York.

McCormick & Company Gains National Distribution Through Acquisition Of A. Schilling & Co., Producers Of Spices And Extracts.

THE HALOID COMPANY ACQUIRES LICENSE FOR NEW PROCESS CALLED ELECTROPHOTOGRAPHY (XEROGRAPHY) FROM BATTELLE MEMORIAL INSTITUTE.

Which senior will you be watching on Graduation Day?

NOTE TO PROUD PARENTS: *For more than 50 years, America's most-desired graduation gift has been a superlatively beautiful and faithfully accurate Hamilton . . . The Fine American Watch.*

BEST ATHLETE. If he's the active, outdoor type, who likes gifts that not only look well but *last* —he'll go for the masculine good looks of a rugged, reliable Hamilton such as the ENDI-COTT (below)—17 jewels, 10K natural gold-filled case. . **$52.25**

MOST POPULAR. Is she constantly in demand—always dashing from one place to another? She needs the steady accuracy of a fine Hamilton like the CLARA, shown below: 17 jewels, 14K natural gold-filled case and snake chain bracelet. . . **$60.50**

MOST LIKELY TO SUCCEED. Is he a born leader. a natural executive? Help him get off to a better start with The Fine American Watch created by skilled American craftsmen. Below is the DONALD—19 jewels, 14K natural gold case. . . . . . **$96.**

CAMPUS QUEEN. Is she the freckle-faced little girl who suddenly became a poised and lovely young woman? She'll be even lovelier wearing a breathtakingly beautiful Hamilton like the BER-NICE, below: 17 jewels, 14K natural or white gold case. **$100.**

BEST STUDENT. Does his brilliant college record prove that there are still some brains left in the family? Show him how proud you are with a watch he'll wear with pride all his life. Below is the LESTER—19 jewels, 14K natural gold-filled case. . . . **$66.**

Hamilton
THE WATCH OF RAILROAD ACCURACY

Only American skills and ingenuity could produce such masterpieces of the watchmaker's art. Hamilton's experience building fine railroad watches and navigational timepieces assures the greatest possible accuracy in every size and grade. At better jewelers everywhere. All prices quoted above include Federal Tax. Send for FREE booklet. Hamilton Watch Company, Dept. B-2, Lancaster, Pennsylvania.

SCIENCE & MEDICINE

Admiral Richard E. Byrd Discovers 10 New Mountains, 5 Offshore Islands And Maps 845,000 Square Miles In A Three-Month Exploration Of The Antarctic.

Location Of The North Pole Moved 200 Miles Further North According To The Canadian Mines And Resources Department.

Professor Willard Frank Libby Develops Method For Determining The Age Of Human, Animal And Plant Remains Through The Measurement Of Carbon-14.

New Atomic Power Plant Constructed At Los Alamos Scientific Laboratory In New Mexico.

The U.S. Makes Available Radioactive Isotopes To Foreign Countries For Biological And Medical Research.

Navy Investigation Of Faulty Computer Data Reveals Presence Of A Dead Moth Near A Relay Giving Birth To The Expression "Debugging" The Computer.

BRITISH ESTABLISH THEIR FIRST ATOMIC PILE AT HARWELL.

BRITAIN SETS UP ADVISORY PANEL ON SCIENTIFIC POLICY.

HUNGARIAN/BRITISH PHYSICIST DENNIS GABOR FORMULATES THEORETICAL BASIS OF HOLOGRAPHY.

Thor Heyerdahl Sails From Peru To Polynesia In 101 Days On A Balsa Raft Named The Kon-Tiki To Prove Pre-Incan Indian Migration.

Two perfect answers to the
$64 QUESTION

... and they're both EVERSHARP!

Did you ever see a handsomer pair ... than this EVERSHARP Skyliner Set? Or a pen and pencil that do more for your writing?

EVERSHARP'S big, 14-karat gold Magic Point personalizes your handwriting—with a variety of line and shading that makes your signature *you!* And writes so smoothly it's actually *silent*. Magic Feed prevents ink flooding high in a plane ... so of course at ground level, too.

Matching Repeater Pencil Feeds new points like a machine gun. Sets, designed in gem-like plastic, available in dubonnet, blue, brown, green, gray, black. Compare!

**TUNE IN Phil Baker in "TAKE IT OR LEAVE IT"—CBS, Sunday Nights
and Ann Sothern in "MAISIE"—CBS, Friday Nights**

Give **EVERSHARP**—*and you give the finest!*

© 1947, Eversharp, Inc.

EVERSHARP
Skyliner Set

$8.75
Pen Alone—$5.00
Pencil—$3.75

Service Guaranteed Forever. If Your EVERSHARP Ever Needs Service, We Will Put It In Good Order For 35¢. This Service Is Guaranteed ... Not For Years ... Not For Life ... But Guaranteed Forever!

1947

P.M.S. Blackett Advances Theory That "All Massive Rotating Bodies Are Magnetic."

First Offshore Drilling Rig Set Up In Gulf Of Mexico. A Record 35,000 Wells Are Drilled In The U.S.—Production Meets Domestic Requirements Only.

Meteorologists Propose Weather Forecasts For Motorists To Help Cut Down On The Number Of Highway Accidents Caused By Bad Weather Conditions.

Small Valve Developed At The Army Air Forces' Aero-Medical Laboratory At Wright Field Used To Regulate Flow Of Oxygen Through A Mask Tested Successfully At Bellevue Hospital On Polio Patients.

Scientists Discover That The Reason Cancer Cells Spread So Easily Is Because They Are Not Sticky Like Normal Cells Which Adhere To Each Other And Do Not Break Away.

Laboratory Mice Convulse And Die After Bombardment With Nerve-Wracking Noises.

Laboratory Mice Put On A Diet Of White Bread Are Found To Be More Resistant To Pneumonia Than Mice On Whole Wheat Bread, Casting Doubt On The Benefits Of Eating Unrefined Foods.

Winthrop Chemical Company Develops Salt Substitute Called Neocurtasal To Be Sold In Retail Drug Stores.

MESCALINE, A HALLUCINATORY DRUG, THOUGHT TO BE AN EFFECTIVE TOOL IN UNDERSTANDING MENTAL DISEASE BY TRIGGERING HALLUCINATIONS IN A CLINICALLY CONTROLLED ENVIRONMENT.

YOU GOTTA STOP BUGGING US

A Worldwide Delousing Project Is Being Planned By The U.S. Department Of Agriculture To Help Combat The Spread Of Lice-Borne Epidemics.

BRITISH INVESTIGATORS REVEAL THAT FIRST BORNS ARE LIKELY TO BE THE MOST INTELLIGENT WITH THE INTELLIGENCE LEVEL DROPPING FOR EACH SUCCEEDING CHILD.

Westinghouse Research Laboratories Develops Plastic Glue Highly Resistant To Ice Or Boiling Water And Strong Enough To Support The Weight Of A 200-Ton Locomotive.

UNIVERSITY OF CALIFORNIA AT BERKELEY BUILDS THE NEWEST, MOST POWERFUL ATOM-SMASHER ON EARTH SMASHING THE ATOM INTO 40 PARTICLES CREATING LIGHTWEIGHT ELEMENTS AND COSMIC RAYS.

Arco Idaho Is First City In The United States To Be Powered By A Nuclear Reactor.

Australian Research Study Indicates That Bees Communicate By Odors And Dancing In Their Hives.

The Agriculture Department Discovers That Bottles Of Milk Left In The Sun For As Little As Half An Hour May Rob The Milk Of Its Flavor And Nutritional Values.

Mexico City: Remains of America's earliest known human being with an age estimated at 10,000 to 15,000 years old are discovered through the use of a geophysical prospecting method.

Chuck Yeager First Human Being To Travel Faster Than Speed Of Sound Breaks Sound Barrier At Speed Of Over 600 MPH.

American Scientists Discover Male Fish In The Republic Of Guatemala That Incubates Eggs By Carrying Them In Their Mouth.

NOBEL PRIZES

MEDICINE

Carl F. Cori (U.S.)

Gerty T. Cori (U.S.)

Bernardo A. Houssay (Argentina)

PHYSICS

Sir Edward V. Appleton (Britain)

CHEMISTRY

Sir Robert Robinson (Britain)

MAX PLANCK, German physicist who received the Nobel Prize for revolutionizing physics through development of his fundamental quantum theory, dies at 89.

WHAT A YEAR IT WAS!

The Christmas Gift
for Important Men

• Websters are being specially boxed and Christmas wrapped this year. Boxes of 25, as low as $3.75. Give Websters by the box. A luxurious gift to yourself and to men who are used to the best.

• There are five different sizes of Websters. Each is made of 100% long Havana, bound in top-quality Broadleaf and wrapped in finest Connecticut Shadegrown. Boxes of 25 and 50 in all sizes. Wherever fine cigars are smoked.

WEBSTER CIGARS
EXECUTIVE AMERICA'S TOP CIGAR

Golden Wedding, 15c	Chico, 15c	Queens, 18c	Fancy Tales, 25c	Directors, 35c
Box of 25—$3.75	Box of 25—$3.75	Box of 25—$4.50	Box of 25—$6.25	Box of 25—$8.75

A PRODUCT OF THE WEBSTER TOBACCO COMPANY, INC., NEW YORK

With Less Than 50% Of Americans Brushing Their Teeth Daily, The American Dental Association Recommends Sodium Fluoride Be Used On Children During Check-Ups.

•

Medical Researchers Find The Cause For The Rising Number Of Women With Damaged Enamel On Their Incisors: Opening Bobby Pins With Their Front Teeth.

•

Aspirin Found To Cause Bleeding In Patients Following Tooth Extractions.

•

A New Dental Anesthetic Applied Without The Use Of A Hypodermic Needle Tested On Patients At Loyola University School Of Medicine.

•

Dental Problems Thought To Be One Cause Of Hearing Impairment.

•

Replanting Knocked-Out Teeth Enjoys Success Only In Children, Not Adults.

THE HIGH PRICE OF REMOVING YOUR APPENDIX

Surgeon $150

Hospital Room $230
($23 per day for 10 days which includes bed & board and post surgical extras. Bill must be paid in full before patient leaves hospital)

Put Away The Chocolate, Buddy

Recent Studies Reveal That Overeating, Not Glandular Dysfunction, Is The Cause Of Obesity. So Much For That Excuse.

New Warning Issued That Eating Too Much Fat Leads To Hardening Of The Arteries.

Vitamin A Synthesized By Dutch And American Laboratories.

THE BASIC MEDICINE CHEST

- Glycerine (Earaches)
- Vaseline & Zinc Oxide (Sunburn, Skin Abrasions)
- Hydrogen Peroxide
- Sodium Bicarbonate
- Aspirin
- Aromatic Spirits of Ammonia
- Laxatives & Cathartics

OTHER EQUIPMENT

- Bed Pan
- Rubber Sheet
- Oral & Rectal Thermometers
- Fountain Syringe
- Adhesive Tape
- Ice Bag
- Graduated Medicine Glass
- Bandages
- Absorbent Cotton

The American Medical Association Recommends That Individuals Over 35 Have An Annual Check-Up.

New York University Establishes Its Medical Center And The Nelson Institute Of Environmental Medicine.

Having The Patient Suck On A Baby Bottle Latest Treatment For The Insane.

Emotional Tension Thought To Trigger Sinus Attacks.

Prefrontal Lobotomy Criticized For Resulting In Permanent Loss In Mental Abilities Including The Ability To Cope With Life.

Thumb Sucking Much More Prevalent In Middle Class Children Than Their Lower-Class Counterparts Probably Due To More Parental Restrictions.

A Report In The Journal Of The American Medical Association Recommends That Penicillin Be Given In The Treatment Of Scarlet Fever.

Dentists At The Mayo Clinic Warn That Drinking Lemon Juice Everyday Destroys The Teeth.

Dentists Begin To Use Music As An Anesthetic In Dental Operations.

Grisein, A New Germ Fighter Related to Streptomycin, Discovered By Dr. Selman A. Waksman, The Researcher Who Also Discovered Streptomycin.

Doctors Are Warned That Streptomycin May Injure Ears Resulting In Dizziness, Vertigo And Temporary Or Permanent Loss Of Hearing.

Polio Virus Isolated By Researchers In Stanford University Giving Hope For The Development Of A Vaccine In The Future.

According To English Obstetrician Dr. Grantly Dick Read, The Primary Cause Of Pain In Childbirth Is Fear—Get Rid Of The Fear And, Lo And Behold, The Pain Vanishes.

According To Professor George E. Morgan, Head Of The Pedodontics Department At Marquette University, More Dentists Are Afraid Of Children Than Children Are Afraid Of Dentists.

WHAT A YEAR IT WAS!

1947 ADVERTISEMENT

Plenty of cheer, this New Year

...because our DOCTOR advised us to take Phillips'

SO GENTLE FOR CHILDREN — SO THOROUGH FOR GROWN-UPS

LYMAN ANDERSON

IT'S FULL SPEED AHEAD FOR THEM BOTH
_thanks to this ideal laxative antacid

THERE's nothing sluggish about my happy family *this* New Year! Today Sonny and Dad are bright as a new dime . . . because last night they needed and took genuine Phillips' Milk of Magnesia. It worked like a charm.

They slept soundly all through the night, without discomforts of acid indigestion. And this morning they awoke to gentle, effective relief from sluggishness.

Mothers, help *your* family face the New Year *bright*. Get Phillips' Milk of Magnesia. The big 50¢ size contains three times as much as the 25¢ bottle. Genuine Phillips' Milk of Magnesia is also available in handy tablet form; 25¢ a box, less than 1¢ a tablet. At all drug stores. Get Phillips' *today*.

GENUINE
PHILLIPS'
MILK OF MAGNESIA
ANTACID   LAXATIVE
SHAKE WELL BEFORE USING

PHILLIPS'
MILK OF MAGNESIA
30 TABLETS

PHILLIPS' WORKS THESE 2 WAYS OVERNIGHT

1 As an acid stomach alkalizer, Phillips' is one of the fastest, most effective known.

2 As a laxative, gentle Phillips' can be taken any time without thought of embarrassing urgency. Caution: Use only as directed.

PHILLIPS'
MILK OF MAGNESIA
Liquid or Tablets

81

Now Skippy, Tell Me About Your Puppyhood

Experimental Open-Heart Surgery Performed On Dogs.

Psychiatry is being explored by the American Veterinary Medical Association as a means of treating dogs suffering from nervous disorders.

Strong Evidence Is Presented In The Psychiatric Quarterly Supporting The Existence Of Telepathic Dreams.

According To Swiss Psychologist, Miss Franziska Baumgarten-Tramer, Chronic Bad Luck Is The Result Of A Mental Defect She Calls "Dusty Thinking," The Victims Of Which Cannot Mentally Focus Their Thoughts Or Actions. Prevention Is Possible By Giving School Children Exercises In Practical Thinking.

AMERICA'S NUMBER 1 HEALTH MENACE—MENTAL DISEASE

Prolonged Mental Illness Thought To Cause Permanent Damage To The Eyes Such As Blurry Vision.

Finger Painting Believed To Be A Successful Tool In Treating Patients With Mental Disorders As Choice Of Colors Reveals Important Personality Characteristics.

New Electric Shock Treatment To The Brain Restores Mental Health To The Extremely Depressed.

According To A University Of Pennsylvania Professor Of Psychiatry, One Out Of Every 140 Americans Is Perfect Which Means One Million People Have No Anxiety, Fears, Vices, Weaknesses Or Prejudices And Have A Long Life Expectancy.

DOCTOR INTRODUCES WEIGHT-LIFTING FOR POLIO PATIENTS

☞ **New Hope In The Treatment Of Syphilis After Penicillin Found To Prevent And Cure Syphilis In Rabbits In Laboratory Experiments.**

☞ **Asthma Attacks Reduced By Radium Treatment.**

☞ **Asthma Symptoms Relieved With Increased Food Consumption.**

☞ **Newly-Developed Mumps Vaccine Tested On 1,000 West Indians.**

10% OF ALL AMERICANS SUFFER SOME HEARING IMPAIRMENT

WHAT A YEAR IT WAS!

I never should have said...
"What kind of Kleenex do you want?"

NOW I've heard everything! jeered the little woman. Maybe you think *all* tissues are Kleenex, but my *skin* says different! If *you* had a faceful of makeup to wrestle with, you'd insist on a plenty *soft* tissue—and you'd *know* there's no other kind of Kleenex!

Clowning again snorted Sue's mother. And with me sneezing cold germs all over. Young man, to hear you talk a body'd think Kleenex was just like *any* tissue. Well, my *nose* knows there's *only one* Kleenex. You'll learn—when these sniffles catch up with you!

It's a greenhorn you are about tissues, sir—meaning no offense! our Nora whispered. Now what other tissues comes poppin' up so handy-like—one at a time? *None but Kleenex!* 'Tis by that fine Kleenex box you'd be knowin' there's only *one* Kleenex. But whish-h-t! —there's still another way...

Your eyes tell you! Hold a Kleenex Tissue up to a light. See any lumps, or weak spots? Divil a bit! You see Kleenex *quality* come smilin' through—pure-as-an-angel—so you're sure that Kleenex *must* be *heavenly soft*. And *husky*, too. Faith, your own eyes tell you there's no other tissue just like Kleenex!

Now I know better...
There is only one KLEENEX

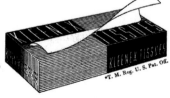

T. M. Reg. U. S. Pat. Off.

America's Favorite Tissue

ONE OF THE FIRST BONE BANKS IS ESTABLISHED IN THE UNITED STATES TO PROVIDE A SUPPLY OF BONE FOR GRAFTING OPERATIONS.

Only One Woman In About 250 Are Color Blind.

VENEREAL DISEASE STILL NATIONAL HEALTH PROBLEM

* 13-Year Old Girl Found To Be Originating Source Of Venereal Infection In 32 Men And Women;

* Three Million Americans Have Syphilis;

* Ten Million Americans Have Gonorrhea;

* Number Of American Soldiers Infected In Europe Highest In Our Military History.

Dr. Eugene Hand Poses Theory That Circumcision Could Prevent Venereal Disease.

1947 ADVERTISEMENT

CHEWING GUM COUGH DROPS

ONLY **COUGH-LETS** GIVE YOU THIS DOUBLE-ACTION RELIEF !

1. **TASTY MEDICATION** (Cough-lets X Formula) soothes!

2. **CHEWING** keeps your throat moist longer!

FOR **BUZZ-SAW** THROAT... *Chew* PLEASANT TASTING...

Cough-lets
DOUBLE-ACTION
MEDICATION SOOTHES · CHEWING KEEPS THE THROAT MOIST
CHEWING GUM COUGH DROPS
Cough-lets CHEWING GUM COUGH DROPS

10¢

Safe for Children!

G. P., INC. 1947

*Use at least half a box of Cough-lets. Then if you don't agree they give you longer-lasting relief than ordinary cough drops, send us the box with the unused contents, and a letter stating your reasons, and we'll cheerfully refund *double* your purchase price.

GUM PRODUCTS, INC., 150 ORLEANS ST., EAST BOSTON 28, MASS.

1947 ADVERTISEMENT

PUT THE ROUND PEG IN WHAT HOLE ?

- **The Average Mental Patient's I.Q. Is Eight Points Below His Normal Counterpart.**

- **Alcoholics And Neurotics Rate Highest Intellectually—Epileptics And Syphilitics Among The Lowest.**

- **According To An Expert Physiologist, The Meek Person Is Abnormal Mentally While The More Aggressive Person Is Normal Showing Better Brain Waves.**

Hundreds Of Thousands Of Disease Carrying Mosquitoes Find Their Way Into The United States From Pacific Islands Via Tires, Shell Cases And Amphibious Vehicles Returning From Combat Areas.

MAKE A FACE, LOSE A PIMPLE

A Report Appearing In The New England Journal Of Medicine Indicates That Facial Exercise Is An Effective Method Of Treating Acne.

Meprane, New Synthetic Hormone To Help Women Through The Discomfort Of Middle Age Transition, Developed By Reed & Carnrick Institute For Medical Research In Jersey City.

A Warning Is Issued By The National Cancer Institute That Radiation Related Illnesses Pose Greatest Threat To Women With Cancer Of The Ovaries Being The Number One Danger.

Benzedrine, Known As "Pep Pills" Successfully Used To Lessen Pain Of Childbirth.

Fatal Blood Clots Which Form After Operations Or Childbirth May Be Prevented By Using Heparin, A Chemical Which Thins The Blood.

X-Ray Treatment Proves Effective In The Treatment Of Arthritis.

The Bronchoscope To Be Used In Detecting Lung Cancer By Sucking

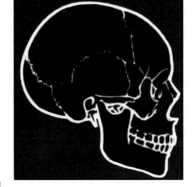

Out Microscopic Pieces Of Tissue For Analysis.

Chronic Diarrhea Relieved By Excluding Milk And Milk Products From The Diet.

Heart Attacks Which Strike During Sleep State Thought To Be Triggered By Bad Dreams.

Sleep Deprivation Causes Symptoms Of Schizophrenia Such As Hallucinations And Irrational Conversations.

VOO DOO SOMETHING TO ME

Despite the increasing acceptance of psychiatry, many people continue to believe that it is
- concerned primarily with sex;
- composed of far-fetched theories about human behavior;
- practiced by disreputable doctors who engage in semi-occult rituals.

INVENTIONS 1947

Dr. Edward Land Introduces The Polaroid Land Camera Which Produces A Picture Within 60 Seconds.

★ The Raytheon Company Introduces Its Microwave Oven.

★ B.F. Goodrich Invents The Tubeless Tire Which Automatically Seals Small Punctures.

★ A Device For Measuring The Speed Of Cars Is Developed.

★ The Zoom Lens Is Developed For Television, 16mm And 35mm Cameras.

★ Piston Core Sampler Is Invented For Ocean-Floor Drilling.

★ The United States Air Force Launches Airplane Piloted By A Robot.

★ The First Military Rescue Helicopter Takes To The Skies.

★ Bell Laboratories Invents The Transistor.

WELL AIN'T THAT THE CAT'S MEOW

Frustrated by frozen sand which made it impossible for her cat to go potty outdoors, a cat owner visited her friendly neighborhood building supply center in Cassoplis, Michigan and asked owner, Ed Lowe, for his help. Ed sold her a bag of industrial absorbent to try in her cat box and lo and behold "Kitty Litter" was born. No longer would our furry, feline friends have to brave the cold winter's chill but could now dispose of their bodily wastes in the warm comfort of their homes. A *purrrr*fect solution!

The Flowers That Bloom In The Spring, Tra La

Two new strands of flowers are introduced:

 RED PINOCCHIO: A dark red velvety double flower, two to three inches across, with a gentle fragrance.

 WHITE WINGS: This five-petal single blossom flower with moderate fragrance and white petals appears in large clusters.

 WHAT A YEAR IT WAS!

87

1947 ADVERTISEMENT

Doctors Prove 2 out of 3 Women can have *Lovelier Skin in 14 days!*

¹"I coaxed, I chided, I cajoled my mirror," says Ruth Cliffe of Inglewood, Calif. "But it was no use. The complexion it showed me stayed dull, dingy and coarse-looking. I don't need to tell you that life's no whirl for a girl with a complexion like that!

"Then the Palmolive Plan came into my life! During a telephone conversation, a friend of mine urged me to try it. She told me how 36 doctors—leading skin specialists—tested this Plan on 1285 women and proved it can bring a lovelier complexion to 2 out of 3 ... in just 14 days!

"Here's all you do: Wash your face with Palmolive Soap.

Then, for 60 seconds, massage with Palmolive's soft, lovely lather. Rinse!

Do this 3 times a day for 14 days. This cleansing massage brings your skin Palmolive's full beautifying effect. Just 14 days after I started the Palmolive Plan, my complexion was fresher, brighter—noticeably finer looking, too!"

YOU, TOO, may look for these skin improvements in only 14 days!

Less Oily . . . .
Smoother, Younger looking.
Less Coarse-looking . . . .
Fewer Tiny Blemishes—
Less Incipient Blackheads .
Fresher . . . .
Brighter, Clearer Color . .

IF you want a complexion the envy of every woman—the admiration of every man—start the 14-Day Palmolive Plan tonight!

Remember, the Palmolive Plan was tested on 1285 women of all ages—from fifteen to fifty—with all types of skin. Dry! Oily! Normal! Young! Older! And 2 out of 3 of these women got noticeable complexion improvement in just 14 days! No matter what beauty care they had used before.

Reason enough for every woman who longs for a lovelier complexion to start this new Beauty Plan with Palmolive Soap!

For tub and shower, get the new, Big, Thrifty Bath Size Palmolive—enjoy Palmolive's soft, lovely lather all over!

PALMOLIVE

DOCTORS PROVE PALMOLIVE'S BEAUTY RESULTS!

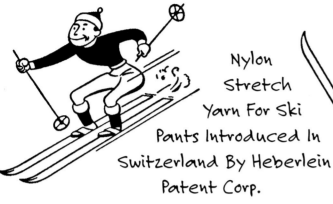

Nylon Stretch Yarn For Ski Pants Introduced In Switzerland By Heberlein Patent Corp.

Lurex, A New Metal Fiber Developed By Eastman Kodak, Aluminum Company Of America And Dobeckmum Introduced To The Textile World.

⭐ Flipper Pinball Machines Are Invented.

⭐ Artificial Leg Testing Machine Developed At Northwestern University That Can Walk 3 Million Miles In Ten Days. Results Of This Testing Will Lead To The Development Of More Efficient Artificial Limbs For The 20,000 Veterans And 65,000 War Workers Who Have Had Amputations.

⭐ Vaccinating Gun Developed By Francis J. Swanson Of Saratoga, Wyoming.

⭐ The Navy Develops Electronic Photo-Flash Which, Flashing At 3-Second Intervals, Is Capable Of Firing 10,000 Flashes On A Single Battery.

⭐ Inventors Reach Most Productive Years In Their 30's And 40's.

⭐ Elderly People Who Suffer Broken Hips Can Now Have Their Shattered Bones Put Back In Place Through The Use Of A Device Known As The Jewett Nail.

⭐ Robert E. Naumberg Invents The Visagraph, A Machine That Converts Ordinary Black On White Print Into Oversized Letters Giving New Hope To The Education, Reading And Advancement For The Blind.

⭐ General Electric Announces The Development Of An Automatic Flight Recorder Designed To Provide Data To Help In Determining The Cause Of Aircraft Mishaps.

The Long-Playing Record Is Invented By Columbia Records' Dr. Peter Goldmark.

 Fireproof Silk Made From Seaweed Introduced To The Textile Industry.

 Cable Device For Sounding A Fire Alarm Is Invented By D.R. Wheeler Of Shreveport, La.

 Bausch & Lomb Optical Company Develops First Trivision Lens For Three-Dimensional Photography.

The Western Union Telegraph Company Installs The First Push-Button System Of Sending Telegrams Which Triples Its Sending Capacity Ushering In A New Era Of Telegraphy.

The Manhattan Rubber Division, Raybestos-Manhattan, Inc., Develops "Easy-Hold" Bowling Ball With A Rubber Cushion Around The Thumb Hole.

A NEW ELECTRONIC STOPWATCH DEVELOPED AT YALE UNIVERSITY MEASURES ONE BILLIONTH OF A SECOND.

• **The U.S. Army Develops The L-13, A Plane Equipped With Folding Wings And Adjustable Landing Gear That Can Fly, Land In The Snow Or Float In The Water.**

• **New Device Developed By Square D Company Will Warn Pilots Of A Developing Stall Enabling Them To Make Corrections.**

Frank L. Folis Of Memphis Invents "Juke-Box" Meals—A System Whereby You Can Order Food Directly From Your Booth By Punching In The Food Number Much The Same Way You Select A Recording From The Juke Box.

✓ *Bertrand H. Wait, Of New Rochelle, New York Invents Salted Cinders To Replace Sand In The Treatment Of Icy Roads.*

✓ *Two Swedish Inventors Develop A One-Piece Telephone That Doesn't Require A Cradle.*

✓ *New Lens Developed That Allows Camera Operator To Instantly Switch From Long Shots To Close-Ups.*

✓ *New Duplication Method Can Mass Reproduce Text Or Drawings At Mimeograph Speed.*

✓ *New Web Press Capable Of Printing 20 Pages Of Color "Funnies" Granted A U.S. Patent.*

✓ *The Tucker Car, A Rear-Engine Sedan With Disk-Type Brakes, Luggage Compartment Under The Hood, And A Windshield That Breaks Free For Safety On Impact Is Designed By Preston Tucker.*

✓ *A New Type Of Facsimile System Is Developed That Allows Color Pictures To Be Received In The Home Or Office By Transmitting Via Wire Or Radio Waves.*

✓ *Using The VT Fuse, A Military Secret During The War, Motion Detection By A Microwave Transmitting-Receiving Unit Is Used By General Electric To Monitor The Movement Of Laboratory Personnel.*

PASSINGS

Frederic W. Goudy, prolific American type designer.

Eric Gill, inventor of Gill Sans, the national typeface of England, dies at 65 of lung cancer.

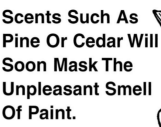

Scents Such As Pine Or Cedar Will Soon Mask The Unpleasant Smell Of Paint.

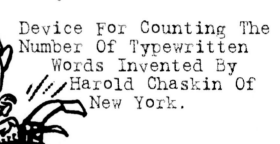

The First Talking Typewriter Which Tells You What Key You've Hit Is Developed By George Coffey.

Device For Counting The Number Of Typewritten Words Invented By Harold Chaskin Of New York.

The Amazing New Automatic way to play records.

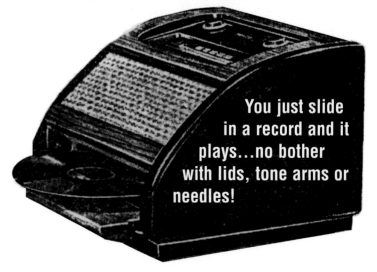

You just slide in a record and it plays...no bother with lids, tone arms or needles!

MEN SHOT FROM GUNS

● A turbo jet, thrusting an airplane ahead at fantastic speed, leaves a trail of new problems reaching straight back to the research laboratory. How efficient is the power plant? Is fuel wasted? How much?

These are questions of first importance—the turbo jet is a glutton for fuel. Shell scientists, trying to get the answers, experienced some of the confusion and distraction of "men shot from guns." They had to invent new methods—conventional laboratory techniques were lost in the hurricane of speed . . .

They succeeded. They have traced down fuel losses with an accuracy measured in tenths of one per cent, circulated their findings and the news of "how to do it" to the Army, Navy, and turbo jet manufacturers. In this exclusive group the news created a stir!

For if the turbo jet's usefulness is to be extended beyond short range fighters—to military planes of longer range, and commercial aviation—the first, essential step is to get every possible mile out of every drop of fuel.

In the inferno of the combustion chamber, air mixes with the gases of burning fuel—the ratio of air to fuel ranging from 45 to 1, to 200 to 1. The blast of the burned air-fuel mixture shoots from the jet at terrific speed.

Shell scientists' problem: capture a "sample" of the exhaust gases. Analyze them to determine ratio of air to fuel. Then, out of the gases, capture the *unburned* fuel, measure the amount.

Their method of getting a sample was successful from the start—and they have since cut the time required for analysis from 3 hours down to 10 minutes! . . . This practically amounts to "continuous recording" of combustion efficiency.

Accurate measurement of fuel losses in turbo jets is only one research achievement by which Shell demonstrates leadership in the petroleum industry, and in petroleum products. Wherever you see the Shell name and trade mark, Shell Research is your guarantee of quality.

**Out of leadership in Research
. . . Shell Premium Gasoline**

You share the advancing knowledge of Shell scientists with every purchase of Shell Premium Gasoline.

SHELL

Horizons widen through Shell Research

© 1947, SHELL OIL COMPANY
Incorporated

NEW PRODUCTS

MSG Marketed For The First Time Under The Brand Name Ac'cent

Whirlpool Brand Introduced To Consumers

Disposable Plastic Baby Bottles Hit American Drug Stores

FIRST HARD-WATER DETERGENT HITS THE MARKET

Reddi-Wip Whipped Cream Is First Major Aerosol Food Product In The United States

Toni Home Permanent Introduces The Toni Twins

FLORIDA INTRODUCES CONCENTRATED FROZEN ORANGE JUICE TO THE AMERICAN CONSUMER.

1947 ADVERTISEMENT

"LOVELY COLORS"

"IT DOESN'T SCUFF"

"NEEDS NO WAXING"

"ALWAYS STAYS NEW LOOKING"

Koroseal Floors are here!

● Now you can have **floors** with all the beauty and labor saving advantages of the same modern "miracle" material used in all Koroseal products. Koroseal floors are virtually indestructible. They stand heat, cold, dryness and dampness. They won't buckle or crack or rot. They resist stains and sun-fading. They are oilproof, acidproof, greaseproof and practically wearproof.

Quiet and easy underfoot, they can be installed over any type of floor or used **as a floor** in new houses. Koroseal floors are perfect for stores, offices, display rooms or any place where traffic is heavy and smart appearance is essential. Koroseal floors have no pores to collect dirt or germs and never get old-looking.

That's Koroseal, your **dream of a floor** — come true!

"CHEAPEST IN THE LONG RUN"

Flooring Specialists since 1807 • Linoleum • Asphalt • Koroseal • Felt Base • Floor and Wall Coverings • Plastic Products

Sloane-Blabon
Corporation

295 FIFTH AVENUE • NEW YORK

Koroseal is a registered trademark of The B. F. Goodrich Co. Koroseal flooring is made under the technical super-vision and control of The B. F. Goodrich Co.

94

ENTERTAINMENT

Joan Fontaine is welcomed as she arrives in sunny Cuba with her husband, William Dozier.

The charming Miss Fontaine is surrounded by admiring fans who seek her autograph.

The Hollywood couple decide to do a little sightseeing.

The couple leave on a Caribbean cruise after seeing the local sights.

Thousands show up for the dedication of the Lou Costello, Jr. Youth Foundation in Los Angeles.

Lou addresses the crowd at the opening.

Bud Abbott & Lou Costello Open Play Center In Los Angeles

Already bringing joy and laughter to thousands of young people, Bud and Lou wanted a safe place for children to gather and play.

WHAT A YEAR IT WAS!

Lou Costello dispenses ice-cream—and it's all free!

One for you and one for me.

Sports activities include tennis, softball, basketball & swimming.

Lou referees a boxing match.

And here's the winner!

The referee takes it on the chin.

FILM FAVORITES

A Double Life
Black Narcissus
The Bachelor And The Bobby-Soxer
The Bishop's Wife
Body & Soul
CROSSFIRE
Dark Passage
Daisy Kenyon
Dead Reckoning
The Exile
The Farmer's Daughter
Forever Amber
The Fugitive
Good News
Gentleman's Agreement
Gran Casino
THE HUCKSTERS
It Happened In Brooklyn
It Had To Be You
KISS OF DEATH
Life With Father
Mad Wednesday
Miracle On 34th Street
Monsieur Verdoux
MY FAVORITE BRUNETTE
NIGHTMARE ALLEY
Odd Man Out
One Wonderful Sunday
Out Of The Past
Possessed
Ride The Pink Horse
Road To Rio
SCARED TO DEATH
Song Of The South

TILL THE CLOUDS ROLL BY
Tweety Pie
The Two Mrs. Carrolls

13 RUE MADELEINE
UNCONQUERED
The Woman On The Beach

Announcing THE FINEST ACHIEVEMENT OF THE CAMERA MAKER'S ART

Only Filmo Auto-8 Camera gives you all these features

Magazine-Loading with Tip-Touch Ejector. Takes the fumble out of film interchange.

Swifturn Two-Lens Turret on which matched finders turn with lenses. Instant readiness for near and distant scenes.

Accurate Viewfinder . . . *What you see, you get.*

Two Filmocoted Lenses. ½" F1.9 and 1½" F3.5 in focusing mounts, for near and distant scenes.

Tell-All Lens-Setting Guide. For both color and black-and-white films; for all outdoor conditions.

Five Filmotrue Speeds including slow motion.

Singlepic Release. So you can animate cartoons, titles, maps.

Selfoto Lock. Lets the operator step into the picture.

Pocket Size—easy to carry.

Lifetime Guarantee.

Filmo Auto Load Camera
Uses 16mm film for larger movies. Split-second loading with pre-threaded film magazine. See it at leading photo dealers now.

Filmo Sportster Camera
Loads easily with 8mm film spools, mounts one superb Filmocoted lens which is quickly interchangeable. Prompt delivery.

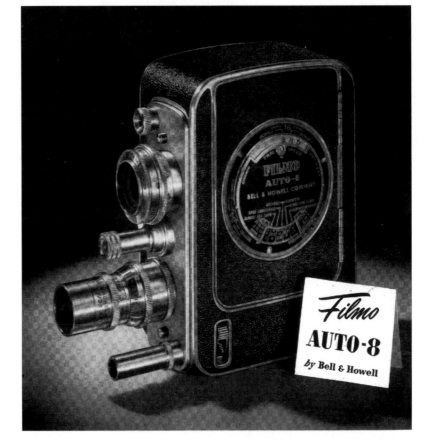

A *new* 8mm magazine-loading movie camera
by the makers of Hollywood's preferred professional equipment

It will make your happiest days even happier . . . this newest and finest of 8mm home movie cameras.

For as you watch those precious scenes through the Filmo Auto-8 viewfinder . . . as you hear the film purr smoothly through this precision-built camera . . . you'll *know* that you're not taking a chance—you're taking a *movie*. A *top-quality* movie that will capture the things you want most to remember—in true-to-life *action* and in full natural color.

You can be *sure* with a Filmo Auto-8 because it is so easy to use correctly . . . and because it fully reflects Bell & Howell's 40 years of experience in building Hollywood's preferred equipment. Only Filmos have this priceless professional heritage.

Leading photographic dealers will be supplied with Filmo Auto-8 as rapidly as possible. For earliest delivery, see your dealer now. And remember, Filmo Auto-8 is worth waiting for. Bell & Howell Company, 7141 McCormick Road, Chicago 45. Branches in New York, Hollywood, Washington, D. C., and London.

Precision-Made by
Bell & Howell
Since 1907 the Largest Manufacturer of Professional Motion Picture Equipment for Hollywood and the World

The Oscar Awards For 1947

(For 1946 Films)

"And The Winner Is..."

BEST PICTURE
The Best Years Of Our Lives

BEST ACTOR
FREDRIC MARCH,
The Best Years Of Our Lives

BEST ACTRESS
OLIVIA DE HAVILLAND,
To Each His Own

BEST DIRECTOR
WILLIAM WYLER,
The Best Years Of Our Lives

BEST SUPPORTING ACTOR
HAROLD RUSSELL,
The Best Years Of Our Lives

Fredric March

BEST SUPPORTING ACTRESS
ANNE BAXTER,
The Razor's Edge

BEST SONG
"On The Atchison, Topeka And Santa Fe"
The Harvey Girls

1947 Favorites *(Oscars Presented In 1948)*

BEST PICTURE
Gentleman's Agreement

BEST ACTOR
RONALD COLMAN, *A Double Life*

BEST ACTRESS
LORETTA YOUNG, *The Farmer's Daughter*

BEST DIRECTOR
ELIA KAZAN, *Gentleman's Agreement*

BEST SUPPORTING ACTOR
EDMUND GWENN, *Miracle On 34th Street*

BEST SUPPORTING ACTRESS
CELESTE HOLM, *Gentleman's Agreement*

BEST SONG
"ZIP-A-DEE-DOO-DAH", *Song Of The South*

Go where you can play this Brilliant NEW WURLITZER!

ZENITH COBRA TONE ARM

Next time you are out for fun and refreshments, go where you can play this brilliant new Wurlitzer Model 1100. Never before have you seen or heard a coin-operated phonograph with so many fun-producing features. Light, color, action! Sensational, moving, ever-changing illumination. Majestic tone that can be regulated to the sound level most pleasing to your taste. There's more *Musical Fun for Everyone* wherever there's one of these colorful, tuneful new Wurlitzers!

WATCH IT IN ACTION

Its panoramic Sky-Top turret window gives you a ringside seat. See the records change and watch Zenith's Cobra Tone Arm play them. This sensational new tone arm eliminates record surface noise—enhances Wurlitzer's famous tone. The music sounds as though the entertainers were right in the room with you.

NEW *Encore* PROGRAM SELECTOR ...is faster, easier—more fun. It rotates 24 popular record titles into view in 3 easy-to-see programs of 8 great tunes each.

Musical Fun for Everyone

The Sign of the Musical Note *identifies places where you can have fun playing a Wurlitzer.*

HOW YOU CAN SEE AND PLAY THIS NEW WURLITZER—*If you would like to see and play this new Wurlitzer in your favorite place for food and refreshments, tell the proprietor to get in touch with his nearest Wurlitzer Music Merchant, or tear out the coupon and ask him to send it to us. We will tell him how he can obtain one of these new Wurlitzers for your entertainment. The Rudolph Wurlitzer Company, North Tonawanda, New York. ★ ★ ★ See Phonograph Section of Classified Telephone Directory for names of Wurlitzer Music Merchants.*

THE RUDOLPH WURLITZER COMPANY
Dept. LA, North Tonawanda, New York

Please tell me how I can provide a new Model 1100 Wurlitzer for the entertainment of my customers.

FIRM NAME

ADDRESS

CITY   STATE   ZONE

Popcorn Anyone?

Decked Out In Finest Evening Attire, Young Women Carry Trays Of Candy Up And Down Aisles Of Movie Theatres Which They Sell During Intermission For The Eating Pleasure Of Patrons.

Hollywood Uses A Helicopter For The First Time To Shoot Two Chase Sequences.

Forever Amber

Breaks First-Day Box-Office Receipts Record, Taking In $25,308.

The Los Angeles Branch Of The Friar's Club Has Its Inaugural Gathering In Beverly Hills With Such Famous Stars In Attendance As JACK BENNY, BOB HOPE and BING CROSBY.

TOP BOX OFFICE STARS

Bing Crosby

Betty Grable

Ingrid Bergman

Gary Cooper

Humphrey Bogart

Bob Hope

Clark Gable

Gregory Peck

Claudette Colbert

Alan Ladd

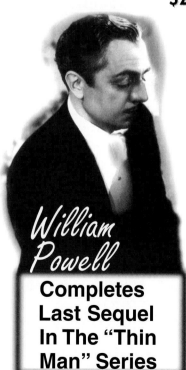

William Powell

Completes Last Sequel In The "Thin Man" Series

Commies In The Movies

George **Murphy** (left) and Screen Actors Guild President **Ronald Reagan** arrive in Washington to testify before the House Un-American Activities Committee Denying Leftists Control Guild.

One of the most outspoken advocates of purging the nation and Hollywood of Communists is **Adolphe Menjou**. Lining up with the majority of the movie industry, he denounces Communist elements and says that in his opinion 95% of Hollywood is comprised of good American citizens.

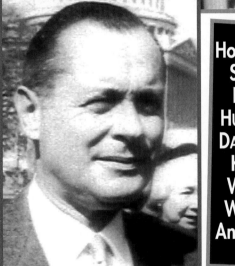

Hollywood Stars Including LAUREN BACALL, HUMPHREY BOGART, DANNY KAYE, GENE KELLY and JANE WYATT Arrive in Washington For Anti-HUAC Protest

George Montgomery with his fellow actors, including **Robert Taylor**, will also testify before the Committee.

Appearing before the inquiry board investigating Communism in the film industry, producer **Sam Wood** wastes no words condemning the Red Party Line and its sympathizers.

HOLLYWOOD TEN Blacklisted By Film Industry

Are You Now Or Have You Ever Been...?

The Committee listens intently to testimony of the various witnesses.

RICHARD WIDMARK Makes Unforgettable Screen Debut In "Kiss Of Death."

•

15-Year Old **FRANÇOIS TRUFFAUT** Forms A Film Club And Meets French Critic Andre Bazin Who Becomes His Mentor.

STARS OF TOMORROW

Janet Blair
Macdonald Carey
Richard Conte
Billy DeWolfe
Claude Jarmon, Jr.
Evelyn Keyes
Peter Lawford
Janis Paige
Gail Russell
Elizabeth Taylor

FINAL CURTAIN

Baron Georg von Trapp, head of famous singing family that fled the Nazis in 1938, dies at 67.

Sidney Toler, best known for his portrayal of Chinese detective Charlie Chan, dies at 74.

FAMOUS BIRTHS

Anne Archer
Meredith Baxter
Glenn Close
Billy Crystal
Tyne Daly
Ted Danson
Richard Dreyfus
Patty Duke
Jill Eikenberry
Farrah Fawcett
Danny Glover
Doug Henning
Kevin Kline
John Larroquette
David Mamet
Joe Mantegna
Tim Matheson
Sam Neill
Edward James Olmos
Mandy Patinkin
Pat Sajak
Jaclyn Smith
Steven Spielberg
Peter Strauss
James Woods

Carmen Finestra

David Letterman

Arnold Schwarzenegger

Gene Autry

MUSIC

1947 POPULAR SONGS

Almost Like Being In Love.......*From "Brigadoon"*

Ballerina......................................*Vaughn Monroe*

Chi-Baba, Chi-Baba ....*Perry Como*

Easter Parade...........................*Guy Lombardo & His Royal Canadians*

Everything I Have Is Yours..................................*Billy Eckstine*

Heartaches ....*Ted Weems & His Orchestra*

Here Comes Santa Claus.......................................*Gene Autry*

I'll Dance At Your Wedding.................................*Buddy Clark*

Linda ....*Ray Noble Orchestra; Buddy Clark, Vocalist*

Near You...*Francis Craig's Band*

On The Atchison, Topeka And Santa Fe...............*From "The Harvey Girls"*

Open The Door, Richard ....*Dusty Fletcher*

Papa, Won't You Dance With Me?........................*Doris Day*

Peg O' My Heart......................*Harmonicats*

Smoke, Smoke, Smoke (That Cigarette) .... *Tex Williams & His Band*

Too Fat Polka ....*Arthur Godfrey*

The Anniversary Song ....*Al Jolson*

Whiffenpoof Song ....*Bing Crosby*

Zip-A-Dee-Doo-Dah ....*From "Song Of The South"*

Al Jolson

FAMOUS BIRTHS

David Bowie

Ry Cooder

Rick Derringer

Barry Gibb

Arlo Guthrie

Emmylou Harris

Elton John

Carole Bayer Sager

Carlos Santana

Laura Nyro

Bob Weir

WHAT A YEAR IT WAS!

1947 ADVERTISEMENT

Intermission ... Have a Coca-Cola

Dancing's fun, but so are those in-between times when you stop and sit one out. That's when it's nice to relax and enjoy *the pause that refreshes* with ice-cold Coca-Cola. *Have a Coke* you say to your partner when the music stops—and you're set for a refreshing and friendly intermission.

* * *

"Coca-Cola" and its abbreviation "Coke" are the registered trade-marks which distinguish the product of The Coca-Cola Company.

Drink *Coca-Cola*

5¢

COPYRIGHT 1947, THE COCA-COLA COMPANY

108

TOP SELLING COUNTRY RECORD
"So Round, So Firm, So Fully Packed"
Merle Travis

Popular Recording Artists

Gene Autry
Pearl Bailey
Victor Borge
Les Brown
Frankie Carle
Buddy Clark
Perry Como
Xavier Cugat
Dennis Day
Doris Day
The Dell Trio
Eddie Duchin
Duke Ellington
Arthur Godfrey
Woody Herman
Lionel Hampton
Harry James
Spike Jones
Beatrice Kay
Gene Krupa
Kay Kyser
Robert Maxwell
The Modernaires
Ray Noble
Harry Owens
Jane Russell
Dinah Shore
Frank Sinatra
The Three Flames

Frank Sinatra

THE STORY OF "RUDOLPH," WRITTEN IN 1939 AND DISTRIBUTED BY MONTGOMERY WARD IN THE FORM OF BOOKLETS, IS SET TO MUSIC FOR THE FIRST TIME.

JIMMY ROGERS & MUDDY WATERS
Pioneer The Chicago Blues Sound

ARISTOCRAT RECORDS Is
Founded By Leonard & Phil Chess

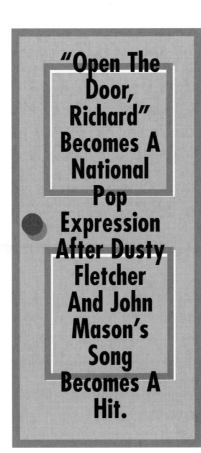

"Open The Door, Richard" Becomes A National Pop Expression After Dusty Fletcher And John Mason's Song Becomes A Hit.

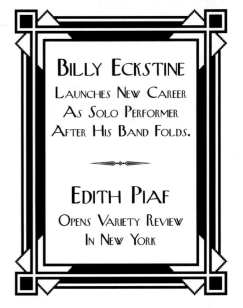

BILLY ECKSTINE
LAUNCHES NEW CAREER AS SOLO PERFORMER AFTER HIS BAND FOLDS.

EDITH PIAF
OPENS VARIETY REVIEW IN NEW YORK

RECORDING STARS OF TOMORROW

Vic Damone
Frankie Laine
Sarah Vaughan

Pulitzer Prize
For Music
CHARLES E. IVES
Symphony No. 3

Classical Music

- **Benjamin Britten's "Albert Herring" Premieres In Glyndebourne**

- **Maria Callas Makes Debut In Ponchielli's "Giaconda" In Verona.**

- **Gottfried von Einem's "Dantons Tod" Opens In Salzburg.**

- **Carl Orff's "Die Bernauerin" Debuts In Stuttgart.**

Gian Carlo Menotti's "The Medium" and "The Telephone" Premiere In New York.

German Opera Producer, Walter Felenstein, Takes Over As Head Of Berlin's Komische Opera.

John Powell Premieres "Symphony In A" In Detroit.

Pablo Casals Vows Not To Perform In Public Until Franco Is Overthrown.

John Cage's THE SEASONS, an experimental composition fusing noise and music and reflecting his interest in Eastern thought, premieres in New York.

New York music critics vote Aaron Copeland's THIRD SYMPHONY best orchestral work.

Dance

George Balanchine's "Theme And Variations" Performed By The American Ballet Theatre At Palais de Cristal In Paris.

WHAT A YEAR IT WAS!

1947 ADVERTISEMENT

A "Royal" gift that will make Christmas last for years!

IMAGINE WAKING UP CHRISTMAS morn and finding . . . a Royal Portable Typewriter—and on the tag, *your name!*

Who wouldn't just *love* such a gift! Especially in those homes where there are young folks of school and college age.

A poll among high school students shows that portable typewriters are among the leaders as a "must" item with teen-agers, and . . .

. . . Royal Portable is their No. 1 choice!

For Royal makes typing *easy!* Royal has many time- and work-saving features

no other portable typewriter can boast of! Here are but a few:

1. The *exclusive* "Magic" Margin, that quickly and easily sets the margin—*automatically!*

2. "Touch Control," which adjusts key tension to *individual speed and touch!*

3. Finger-Flow Keyboard, the *fully* standard "office machine" keyboard!

And Royal Portable is carefully constructed to *last!* Royal is sturdy and rugged! No won-

der Royal Portable is the choice of students!

So make it a Royal Portable this Christmas! It's the best typewriter investment in *anybody's* young life!

ROYAL PORTABLE

The Standard Typewriter in Portable Size

"Magic" and "Touch Control" are registered trade-marks of Royal Typewriter Company, Inc.

111

Exploration of ocean depths is made possible by RCA Image Orthicon television camera.

The ocean is a "goldfish bowl" to RCA Television!

Another "first" for RCA Laboratories, undersea television cameras equipped with the sensitive RCA Image Orthicon tube were used to study effects of the atom blast at Bikini . . .

There may come a day when fishermen drop a television eye over the side to locate schools of fish and oyster beds . . . Explorers will scan marine life and look at the ocean floor . . . Undersea wrecks will be observed from the decks of ships without endangering divers.

With the new television camera, long-hidden mysteries of the ocean depths may soon be as easy to observe as a goldfish bowl—in armchair comfort and perfect safety.

Exciting as something out of Jules Verne, this new application of television is typical of research at RCA Laboratories. Advanced scientific thinking is part of any product bearing the name RCA, or RCA Victor.

When in Radio City, New York, be sure to see the radio and electronic wonders at RCA Exhibition Hall, 36 West 49th Street. Free admission. *Radio Corporation of America, RCA Building, Radio City, New York 20.*

Through RCA Victor home television you will see not only the best in entertainment and sports, but educational subjects . . . the latest news . . . and "history as it happens." If you are in a television area, ask your dealer to demonstrate the new RCA Victor home television sets.

 RADIO CORPORATION of AMERICA

1947

The hastily scheduled **Howdy Doody Show** with host Buffalo Bob premieres on December 28 with only the voice of the not quite constructed puppet heard by audiences.

William Paley Recognizes The Extraordinary Potential Of Television And Moves Ahead To Develop Programming For ABC.

PRIME TIME TELEVISION PROGRAMS

AMERICANA

BIRTHDAY PARTY

CAMPUS HOOPLA

CHARADE QUIZ

DOORWAY TO FAME

EYE WITNESS

GILLETTE CAVALCADE OF SPORTS

KRAFT TELEVISION THEATRE

MARY KAY AND JOHNNY

MUSICAL MERRY-GO-ROUND

SMALL FRY CLUB

WESTERN MOVIE

YOU ARE AN ARTIST

Television Networks Outscoop Movie Theatre Newsreels By Four Days By Flying In Footage Of The Royal Wedding Between Princess Elizabeth And Philip Mountbatten, Duke Of Edinburgh.

Gorgeous George Becomes Bleached Blond Star Of DuMont Network's Wrestling Matches.

178,571 Television Sets Are Manufactured This Year vs. 6,476 Last Year.

NBC Votes To Ban Crime Shows Before 9:30 P.M.

1947

⟫ **ABC, NBC, CBS And DuMont Television Networks Broadcast Up To 30 Hours Of Live Programming Weekly. DuMont Introduces Kinescope—A Method Of Recording Programs.**

⟫ **Television Evolves From Experimental Technology To An Established Broadcasting Service.**

⟫ **The Opening Session Of Congress Is Televised For The First Time.**

⟫ **"Small Fry Club" Debuts As First Children's Series And First Program To Be Broadcast Five Days A Week.**

⟫ **"Kraft Television Theatre" Debuts And Advertises New Product, Imperial Cheese, Which Sells Out Within Three Weeks In New York City.**

⟫ **The First Evening News Shows Debut—"CBS Evening News" Introducing Douglas Edwards, and DuMont Presents "News From Washington" With Walter Compton.**

⟫ **For The First Time Millions Of Baseball Fans Watch The World Series On Television Sets In Their Homes, Department Stores And Bars.**

RADIO

The "Who's On First" Routine Airs For The First Time On THE ABBOTT & COSTELLO SHOW

BUCK and KILLER KANE fight their last battle as BUCK ROGERS IN THE TWENTY-FIFTH CENTURY ends after 15 years.

WHAT A YEAR IT WAS!

ALLEN FUNT'S "Candid Microphone" Hits ABC Radio Airwaves

TOP 10 NETWORK RADIO PROGRAMS 1947

BOB HOPE
JACK BENNY
FIBBER MCGEE & MOLLY
CHARLIE MCCARTHY
AMOS 'N' ANDY
FRED ALLEN
RED SKELTON
RADIO THEATRE
MR. DISTRICT ATTORNEY
TRUTH OR CONSEQUENCES

➲ **93% Of U.S. Households Own Radios.**

➲ **Memphis Introduces First All-Black Programming Station.**

➲ **The FCC Grants First Citizens Band (CB) Radio License.**

➲ **Dorothy Fuldheim Becomes Nation's First News Anchorwoman On Cleveland's WEWS-TV.**

NEW RADIO PROGRAMS 1947

You Bet Your Life
GROUCHO MARX

The Jack Paar Show

Lassie
MARVIN MILLER

Strike It Rich
TODD RUSSELL

My Friend Irma
MARIE WILSON

Stop Me If You've Heard This One
ROGER BOWER

You Are There
DON HOLLENBECK

Art

Jacob
Lawrence
"Dancing Doll"
✳
Edward
Hopper
"Pennsylvania Coal Town"
"Summer Evening"
✳
William
Baziotes
"Dwarf"
✳
George
Braque
"Still Life"
✳
Stuart
Davis
"Iris"
✳
Charles
Sheeler
"Classic Still Life"
✳
Jackson
Pollock
"War"
"Full Fathom Five"
✳
Arshile
Gorky
"The Betrothal II"
"Agony"
✳
Stephen
Greene
"The Deposition"
"The Burial"
✳
Willem
de Kooning
"Noon"

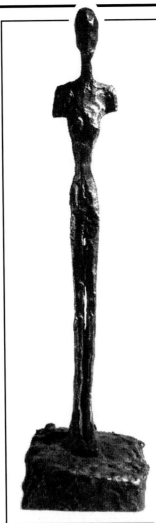

Alberto
Giacometti
"The Pointing Man"
sculpture
"Standing Woman"
painting

Pepsi-Cola's Exhibition For American Artists

MAX WEBER
"Flute Soloist" $2,500 1st Prize

LAMAR DODD
"The Breaker" $2,000 2nd Prize

YOU CALL THIS ART?

Over loud protests from the professional art world, "Advancing American Art," a traveling exhibit of 79 American modern art paintings, is recalled from Czechoslovakia by Secretary Of State Marshall after members of Congress denounced the works as ugly and un-American.

The Jewish Museum, The First Of Its Kind In The United States, Opens In New York Housing Ancient And Modern Works.

Chrysler Joins The Encyclopedia Britannica, Pepsi-Cola And Gimbels As Industrial Patrons Of The Arts.

The First Book Printed In The United States— The Bay Psalm Book (1640)—Sells for $151,000.

GERMAN PAINTER MAX BECKMANN COMES TO THE U.S. TO TEACH MODERN ART AT WASHINGTON UNIVERSITY IN ST. LOUIS.

PRINTS
Announcing a vitally important
CATALOG for PICTURE LOVERS
98-page illustrated catalog with a listing of practically every available reproduction of OLD MASTERS, MODERNS & CONTEMPORARIES—foreign & American.
Mailing Chgs.: 25c. U. S. ... 30c. Canada
Mail orders and inquiries promptly handled

Oestreicher's
1206 6th Ave. (Dept. T)   New York 19
(Bet. 47th-48th Sts.)   BR. 0-1143

15 NEW ARTISTS in POST-WAR JAPAN
to June 5
Tribune SUBWAY Gallery
100 W. 42 St. (Sub. Arcade Downstairs)
Ask For Catalogue
232 pp., 59 color & 663 other repro.

PAINTINGS OF PARIS by
GABRIEL SPAT
APRIL 29th THROUGH MAY 17th 1947
Carroll Carstairs Gallery
11 East 57th Street, New York 22, N.Y.

Recent Paintings
MOTHERWELL
● KOOTZ 15 E. 57

LANDSCAPE
PAINTINGS OF
FOUR CENTURIES
Through May
KOETSER ● 32 E. 57 ST.

ELENA PIÑERO DE MÜLLER
VENEZUELAN PAINTER
May 6th—9 P. M.
May 7th, 20th—2 to 11 P. M.
Ateneo Cubano, 2824 Broadway, N. Y.

RUTH • TED • CHARLES
PAINTINGS **EGRI**
May 4
May 29
RoKo 51 GREENWICH AVE., N. Y. 1
GALLERY EAST OF 7th AVE. & 11th ST.

EVERYTHING IN ART SUPPLIES
Equalized Spectrum Oil Colors Tubes No. 4"—Complete set of 8 colors and white
$4.00

featuring **DEVOE** ARTISTS MATERIALS
DEVOE PAINT STORES
60 East 42nd St. • 110 Fulton St

American
Art School
3410 BWAY., N.Y. • LO 8-3960
SUMMER CLASSES June 2-Aug. 30
WILLIAM GROPPER
ROBERT PHILIPP
JOSEPH POWERS
GORDON SAMSTAG
Approved for Veterans

Robert
Motherwell
"Western Air"
"The Red Skirt"
✳
Barnett
Newman
"The Euclidean Abyss"
✳
Hans
Hoffman
"Ecstasy"
✳
Alexander
Calder
"Little Red Under Blue"
(sculpture)

WHAT A YEAR IT WAS!

116

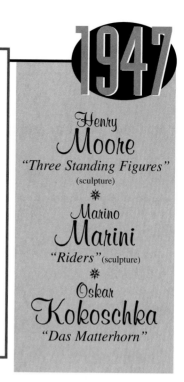

ART PRIZES

Almost every major museum or art institute follows the school of modern art trend and most of the prize-winning paintings and museum acquisitions fall into this catagory. Realism is given little or no consideration.

Arthur Osver "Majestic Tenement"
Pennsylvania Academy of the Fine Arts **Temple Gold Medal Prize**

Philip Guston "Holiday" New York's National Academy of Design **$1,200 Altman Prize**

Eugene Speicher Painter • **Paul Sample** Painter
Marion Sanford Sculptor • **Peter Dalton** Sculptor
New York's National Academy of Design **$1,000 Prize to each**

Zoltan Sepeshy "Marine Still Life"
Pittsburgh's Carnegie Institute **$1,500 First Prize**

Joseph Hirsch "The Iceman" Pittsburgh's Carnegie Institute **$1,000 Second Prize**

William Baziotes "Cyclops" Chicago's Art Institute **$1,000 Campana Purchase Prize**

Rico Lebrun "Vertical Composition" Chicago's Art Institute **$500 Harris Prize**

Henry Kallem "Country Tenement" Pepsi-Cola's Exhibition for American Artists

North Carolina Opens North Carolina Museum Of Art— First State Museum In The United States Funded With Public Money.

Henry **Moore**
"Three Standing Figures"
(sculpture)
✳
Marino **Marini**
"Riders" (sculpture)
✳
Oskar **Kokoschka**
"Das Matterhorn"

British Sculptor Henry Moore's Exhibition At The Museum Of Modern Art Receives Critical Acclaim.

The Wildenstein Galleries In New York Does Full Exhibit Of Mary Cassatt, The U.S. Painter Who Became Part Of The Impressionist Group In France.

French Government Sends Collection Of French Tapestries For Exhibition At The Metropolitan Museum Of Art.

Museum Of Modern Art Does Ben Shahn Retrospective.

Infrared Photography Used To Prove Authenticity Of Old Masters And To Detect Forgeries.

Metropolitan Museum Of Art Exhibits First One-Man Show By Living Artist—Yugoslav Sculptor Ivan Mestrovic.

Jackson Pollock, One Of The Most Outstanding Artists Of The Younger Generation Of American Painters And Considered The Most Important New Painter Since Miro, Exhibits His Fourth One-Man Show At ART OF THIS CENTURY Gallery. Pollock Begins To Use His Drip-Painting Technique, Working With The Canvas Pinned To The Floor Enabling Him To Have More Direct Physical And Emotional Contact With His Work.

Jean Dubuffet Holds His First New York One-Man Show.

Isamu **Noguchi**
"Kouros" (sculpture)
✳
Jose **de Rivera**
"Yellow Black" (sculpture)
✳
William **Zorach**
"The Future Generation"
(sculpture)
✳
Theodore **Roszak**
"The Specter Of Kity Hawk" (sculpture)
✳
Kurt **Seligman**
"Star Eater"
✳
Maurice **de Vlaminck**
"A Bunch Of Flowers"

Henri **Matisse**
"Les Fleurs du Mal"
book illustrations
"Dahlias and Pomegranates" and
"Young English Girl"
paintings

On His First Trip To The United States, JOAN MIRO Accepts Commission For Large Mural For A Cincinnati Hotel.

Pierre Bonnard, One of the great 20th century Impressionist painters, dies at 80 in Cannes.

WHAT A YEAR IT WAS!

books

1947

L.S. Amery
THOUGHTS ON THE
CONSTITUTION

Jean Anouilh
L'INVITATION AU CHATEAU

Thomas Armstrong
KING COTTON

H. E. Bates
THE PURPLE PLAIN

Saul Bellow
THE VICTIM

Nigel Balchin
LORD I WAS AFRAID

Albert Camus
THE PLAGUE

E. F. Carritt
ETHICAL AND POLITICAL
THINKING

G. D. H. Cole
THE INTELLIGENT MAN'S
GUIDE TO THE POST-WAR
WORLD

BETTY CROCKER'S PICTURE
COOKBOOK

Theodore Dreiser
THE STOIC

John Erskine
THE MEMORY OF
CERTAIN PERSONS;
AN AUTOBIOGRAPHY

A. Ewing
LITTLE GATE

Anne Frank
THE DIARY OF
ANNE FRANK

H.W. Garrod
SCHOLARSHIP, ITS
MEANING AND VALUE

Maxim Gorky
MOTHER

Julian Green
SI J'ETAIS VOUS

John Gunther
INSIDE U.S.A.

A. B. Guthrie
THE BIG SKY

Theodor Heuss
DEUTSCHE GESTALTEN

Laura Hobson
GENTLEMAN'S AGREEMENT

William Douglas-Home
THE CHILTERN HUNDREDS

Karl Jaspers
THE QUESTION OF GUILT

Siegfried Kracauer
FROM CALIGARI TO HITLER

Sinclair Lewis
KINGSBLOOD ROYAL

Malcolm Lowry
UNDER THE
VOLCANO

PRIZES

NOBEL

Literature:
ANDRE GIDE

PULITZER

Fiction:
ROBERT PENN
WARREN
All The King's Men

Poetry:
ROBERT LOWELL
Lord Weary's Castle

History:
JAMES PHINNEY
BAXTER III
*Scientists Against
Time*

Journalism:
BALTIMORE SUN

Reporting:
FREDERICK WOLTMAN
*New York
World-Telegram*

**National
Reporting:**
EDWARD T. FOLLIARD
Washington Post

**International
Reporting:**
EDDY GILMORE
Associated Press

Correspondence:
BROOKS ATKINSON
New York Times

**Editorial
Cartooning:**
VAUGHN SHOEMAKER

books

Thomas Mann
DR. FAUSTUS
AND
ESSAYS OF THREE DECADES
(FIRST AMERICAN EDITION)

James Michener
TALES OF THE SOUTH PACIFIC

Robert Payne
THE BEAR COUGHS AT THE
NORTH POLE

Michael Polanyi
SCIENCE, FAITH AND SOCIETY

J. P. Priestley
THE LINDEN TREE

Samuel Putnam
PARIS WAS OUR MISTRESS;
MEMOIRS OF A LOST AND
FOUND GENERATION

Edward Roditi
OSCAR WILDE

Guido Ruggiero
EXISTENTIALISM

Michael Sadlier
FANNY BY GASLIGHT

Jean Paul Sartre
THE AGE OF REASON

Dr. Seuss
MCELLIGOT'S POOL

Mickey Spillane
I, THE JURY

John Steinbeck
THE WAYWARD BUS
AND
THE PEARL

Hugh Trevor-Roper
THE LAST DAYS OF
HITLER

Richard Wright
SELECTED ESSAYS

Frank Yerby
THE VIXENS

FAMOUS BIRTHS

Tom Clancy
Stephen King
Salman Rushdie
Danielle Steele

Maxwell Perkins, editor to F. Scott Fitzgerald, John Phillips Marquand, Ernest Heminway and co-author with Thomas Wolfe of "Look Homeward Angel," dies at 63.

Willa Cather, who chronicled the frontier and won the Pulitzer Prize for her "Death Comes For The Archbishop," dies at 74.

— Dr. Seuss

WITH THE 1947 *Mercury*

The Mercury '47 Town Sedan

More OF EVERYTHING YOU WANT...

Wherever it goes, the '47 Mercury creates a pleasant stir. Drive up, say, to a country club and see how quickly the doorman is ready to take over.

That hood's a honey!

He's not a bad judge of cars—handles all kinds—and likes to drive a Mercury because

it's so easy to park, so *lively*, so responsive to the wheel, the accelerator and the brake.

You'll like it, too. You'll like its sleek, youthful lines...its smooth-flowing contours

Such luxury!

accented with just the right touches of chromium. You'll like its handsomely blended two-toned interior...its super-comfortable

seats that let you stretch out and relax . . . its impressive *big car* look and feel.

What a get-away!

See this new '47 Mercury—with more beauty, more comfort, more "life" and more economy than ever before—now at your nearest Lincoln-Mercury Dealer. It has even *more* of everything you want for '47!

MERCURY—DIVISION OF FORD MOTOR COMPANY

WITH THE 1947 *Mercury*

ON BROADWAY

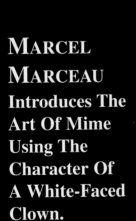

MARCEL MARCEAU Introduces The Art Of Mime Using The Character Of A White-Faced Clown.

ANOTHER OPENING, ANOTHER NIGHT

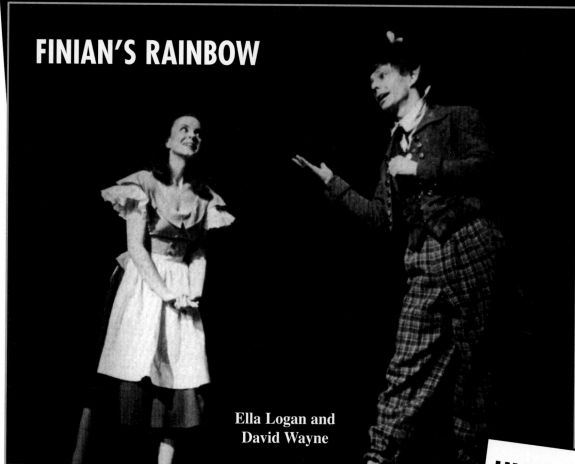

FINIAN'S RAINBOW

Ella Logan and
David Wayne

BRIGADOON
David Brooks and Margaret Bell

HIGH BUTTON SHOES
Phil Silvers and
Nanette Fabray

STREET SCENE
Book: Elmer Rice
Music & Lyrics: Kurt Weill &
Langston Hughes

WHAT A YEAR IT WAS!

Arthur Miller's
ALL MY SONS
Makes U.S. Debut

Ed Begley *(left)* and Arthur Kennedy

Tennessee Williams'
A Streetcar Named Desire

Starring Marlon Brando, Jessica Tandy, Kim Hunter and Karl Malden Stun Audiences And Critics Alike In An Electrifying Broadway Debut.

"Brando, mumbling and cursing in a sweaty undershirt, dominates the stage."

GO TO HECK YOU GOSH DARN BLONDE PORKER SON-OF-A-FEMALE HUSBANDLESS DOG OF THE NIGHT!

Eugene O'Neill's Detroit production of "A Moon For The Misbegotten" was threatened with closure by ever vigilant censors unless certain objectionable words were removed from the script. Thanks to the blue pencil, theatregoers are now spared from such shocking words as "Whore," "Bastard," "God Damn," "Son Of A Bitch" and "Blonde Pig."

Laurence Olivier

Knighted By King George VI For Outstanding Artistic Contribution To Stage And Screen.

The Tony Award Is Established In Memory Of Antoinette Perry Who Headed The American Theatre Wing During World War II.

ANNIE GET YOUR GUN

Banned In Memphis Because Of Integrated Cast.

Edinburgh Inaugurates Its First International Festival Of Music And Drama Attracting "Fringe" Performing Artists Who Perform On Improvised Stages.

- Alan Jay Lerner & Frederick Loewe Enjoy Their First Broadway Success With The Debut Of "Brigadoon."

- Curtain Falls On "Life With Father" After A Record 8-Year Broadway Run.

DISASTERS

Weehawken, N.J. Fire

One of New York Harbor's most spectacular fires rages as a pier at Weehawken, N.J., just opposite mid-town Manhattan, burns to the water's edge.

A Universal cameraman films the inferno as firemen from six New Jersey communities battle the blaze which could be seen for miles.

The pier, which served railroads coming in from the West, is completely destroyed along with cargo awaiting export. Total loss is estimated at 6.5 million dollars.

WHAT A YEAR IT WAS!

Weehawken, N.J. Fire

More than 30 fire-fighting boats from the Coast Guard and harbor fire departments, as well as tugboats, took part in the fight. For a time the fire threatened to become one of the costliest in New Jersey's history.

During the 48 hour fight to bring the fire under control, 12 firemen and pier workers were injured or overcome by smoke.

WHAT A YEAR IT WAS!

1947 ADVERTISEMENT

Handsome lifeguard in daring rescue. Every day, almost, Junior (very) Lifeguard Georgie rescues his "model" mother. It's good fun and exercise. Fortunately, Virginia knows that gums, too, need exercise. Because today's soft foods tend to make them tender and flabby. So the Swensens use Ipana — specially designed, with gentle massage, to help gums to healthier firmness.

This Mother never dreamed of becoming a Model

...until her lovely figure and winning smile won Virginia Swensen a Miami beauty contest

IT'S POSSIBLE that if she hadn't won a beauty contest, Virginia Swensen of Miami Springs might still be modeling aprons in her kitchen . . , instead of fashions in a model agency.

It's possible—but not probable. With her figure, her bright-as-Florida-sunshine smile, she couldn't miss becoming a hit. Today this lovely mother knows more than ever the importance of a smile.

So she's teaching 4-year-old Georgie her own prized dental routine: *Regular brushing with Ipana, then gentle gum massage.*

Until recently a Nurse's Aid, Mrs. Swensen knows what thousands of dentists and schools are teaching today—that a radiant smile depends on sparkling teeth. And sparkling teeth call for firm, healthy gums. So start now toward a "model" smile yourself—with Ipana Tooth Paste.

Giddyap Napoleon! A few more riding lessons and Georgie, a tireless radio fan, will have Snake-Eyes Sanchez biting the dust. But he needs no lessons in care of teeth and gums, "Every time you brush your teeth, massage your gums gently," his mother has taught him. This brief workout with Ipana helps speed up circulation within the gums.

Many parents could learn from their youngsters the importance of gum massage, taught in thousands of schools today. Also, 7 out of 10 dentists recommend gum massage, national survey shows. (And dentists, 2 to 1, prefer Ipana for their own personal use.) But let *your* dentist decide whether and how to massage your gums.

"A lifeguard must be strong," Virginia reminds ambitious Georgie, "with strong teeth and sound gums." Sensitive gums often herald their warning with "pink" on your tooth brush—a sign to *see your dentist*. Let *him* decide whether yours is simply a case for "the helpful stimulation of Ipana and massage."

Product of Bristol-Myers

Start today with Ipana and Massage

127

1947

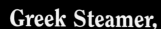

Greek Steamer, "Himera" Hits Mine Off Athens— 392 Die.

French Freighter, "Grandcamp" Explodes In Texas City, Texas Harbor Starting Fires Resulting In Over 500 Deaths.

- **111** Perish In Mine Disaster In Centralia, Illinois.

- **169** Die In Tornado That Sweeps Texas, Oklahoma And Kansas.

- Tidal Wave Strikes Honshu Island, Japan Killing **1,900** People.

Eastern Airlines DC-4 Crashes Near Port Deposit, Maryland Killing 53.

Truman Declares Maine A Disaster Area And Grants Aid In Response To Its $30 Million In Fire Losses.

24 Die In Rail Crash Near Gallitzen, Pennsylvania.

1947 ADVERTISEMENT

Cleaner · Water Heater · Electric Sink · Refrigerator · Home Freezer · Range · Laundromat · Dryer · Radio · Mixer · Fan · Iron · Toaster · Waffle Baker · Table Grill · Warming Pad · Percolator · Comforter · Roaster Oven

★ FAMOUS WESTINGHOUSE ELECTRIC RANGE ★

Who says you have to be **Born** *a good cook!*

Any Cook Can Be Sure of perfect results on the new, 1947 Electric Ranges by Westinghouse. They're so *easy* to use, so *fast*, so *sure* in their uniform cooking results.

Exclusive Tel-A-Glance Switches cut out guesswork. Faster-than-ever Corox units provide right temperatures for all types of surface cooking. The new, fast Deep Well Cooker *now*

deep-fries, steams, boils. Also does most types of surface cooking. Ovens have balanced heat, waist-high broilers.

Beautiful to look at . . . Still more beautiful in Performance, these new Ranges, and many other Westinghouse electric appliances, are on their way to you now. They'll save you endless work. See them at your Westinghouse retailer's.

Every house needs Westinghouse

Maker of 30 MILLION Electric Home Appliances

WESTINGHOUSE ELECTRIC CORPORATION · PLANTS IN 25 CITIES · OFFICES EVERYWHERE · APPLIANCE DIVISION, MANSFIELD, OHIO

Tune in Ted Malone . . . Monday through Friday . . . 11:45 A.M., E.D.T. . . . ABC Network

The winter's worst snow leaves Montreal's cars stranded and motorists with the problem of getting their automobiles started again.

STORM HITS MONTREAL

In Saskatchewan the blizzard driven by winds of 60 miles an hour leaves Regina buried under drifts from 10 to 15 feet deep.

On the prairie outside the city the transcontinental trains of the Canadian National Railroad are stalled in drifts that bury the entire province.

Men and bulldozers make heroic efforts to clear the snow mountain.

A plow is attached to the front of a locomotive traveling 40 miles an hour. After 60 hours, the tracks to Vancouver are cleared.

when your heart cries
STOP!

You must stop. A life depends on it. How good it is to know that you're riding on Fisk Safti-Flights, America's only tire with White Safety Stripes.

The instant you press the brake pedal, hundreds of film-cutting tread blocks automatically go to work. That's the job that Fisk's Safety Stripes do for you.

With Safety Stripes you stop fast. You stop smoothly. You stop straight!

See your Fisk dealer soon. A set of new Fisk Safti-Flights on your car might save a life...tomorrow.

...it's the
STRIPES

TIME TO
RE-TIRE
Rsr. U.S.
Pat. Off.

FISK
Safti-Flight
THE SAFETY STRIPE TIRE

FISK TIRE COMPANY, DIVISION OF UNITED STATES RUBBER COMPANY

FASHION

Dior's NEW LOOK

French designer Christian Dior introduces his first couture collection creating the "New Look" – a radical departure from functional war-time styles when designers had to work with severe shortages of material.

Removing shoulder pads to create a softer look, Dior drops hemlines to within 12 inches of the floor, with suit jackets fitting tightly around the bodice and flaring at the waist.

The "New Look" is greeted enthusiastically by women who love the feminine styling but less so by men who hate the idea of not being able to see their legs.

A tiny waist, tapering shoulders, full three-quarter length skirt and high-heeled court shoes.

1947 ADVERTISEMENT

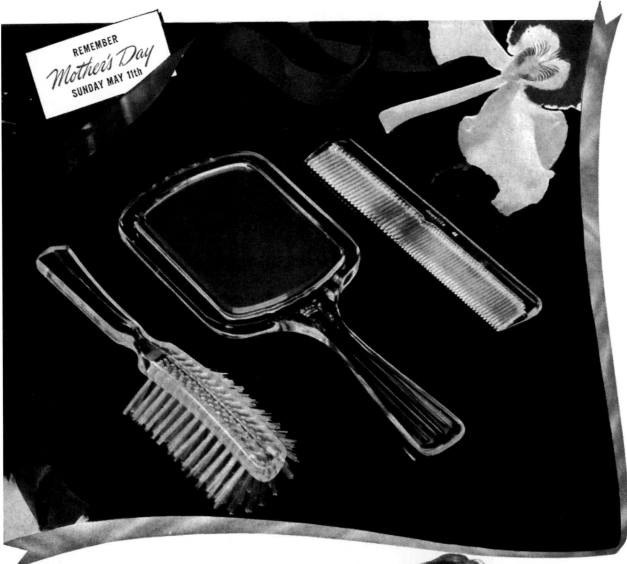

REMEMBER
Mother's Day
SUNDAY MAY 11th

The gift that's a promise of Lovelier hair

Jewelite
by Pro-phy-lac-tic

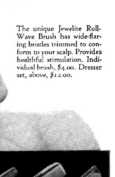

The unique Jewelite Roll-Wave Brush has wide-flaring bristles trimmed to conform to your scalp. Provides healthful stimulation. Individual brush, $4.00. Dresser set, above, $12.00.

● No tribute to Mother could be more gracious than a gift of Jewelite by Pro-phy-lac-tic. Jewelite Brushes, Combs, and complete Dresser Sets, styled in the most beautiful of plastics, are available in delicate shades of ruby or sapphire, as well as in diamond-clear crystal. And every Jewelite Brush has bristles of long, resilient Prolon (finest of synthetic bristle) to help burnish the hair and bring out every natural highlight. Jewelite, sold at good brush departments, is a product of Pro-phy-lac-tic, makers of the famous Pro-phy-lac-tic Tooth Brush. Look for the name Jewelite on the box. PRO-PHY-LAC-TIC BRUSH CO., *Florence, Mass.*

Guaranteed by
Good Housekeeping

Jewelite Combs and other lovely Pro-phy-lac-tic Plastic Combs for men and women are designed for perfect combing. Available in a wide variety of styles and colors. 15¢ to 50¢.

134

Middy top over all-around pleated skirt.

But Madame, Your Ankles Are Showing

Fashion Plate Bettina Wilson, Editor Of Vogue, Was Refused Admittance To London's Snooty "400" Club When She Arrived Dressed In An Up-To-The-Minute Fashionable Paris Creation Falling Just Above The Ankles On The Grounds It Was Improper.

Choose these famous Bretton bands to beautify the watch you wear...

LOOK FOR THEM ON THE FAMOUS WATCH YOU BUY

LEADING watch manufacturers, quick to anticipate fashion trends and public demand, invariably choose fine quality BRETTON bands. Because BRETTON bands flatter, lend distinction to and harmonize with their watches; are splendid jewelry creations in their own right. So look for BRETTON bands when you buy a watch, choose them to beautify the watch you already have. At better jewelers. Bruner-Ritter, Inc., 630 Fifth Avenue, New York, and Montreal.

Bretton
Queen

Exclusive BRETTON creation, noteworthy for its ingenious styling and design, streamlined smartness, flowing beauty. Most popular of all ladies' expansion bands. In white, yellow or pink gold — 14kt. $50; 1/20 12 kt. gold filled, $10.50.

Bretton
Bretweave

Another outstanding example of traditional BRETTON master craftsmanship — and the real thing in men's basketweave watch bands. Created with expansion center or patented Supermatic safety catch. 1/20 12kt. gold filled, $10.50.

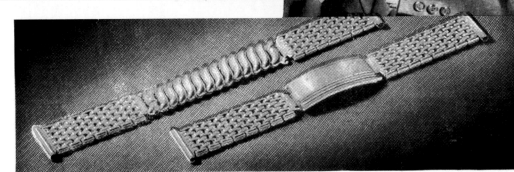

Bretton FIRST AMONG FINE WATCH BANDS

MORE FAMOUS WATCHES WEAR BRETTON BANDS THAN ANY OTHER KIND

Copyright 1947, Bruner-Ritter, Inc.

The New Look

A two-piece suit with a trimmer, cleaner line with hipline built out with horsehair.

A triple-tiered one-piece dress with cape sleeves.

A dress that can be worn for late afternoon and evening has a swooping skirt that dips gracefully to the back of the ankle.

A pleated one-piece tier dress.

WHAT A YEAR IT WAS!

Dress with brief shoulder cape.

Dress with detachable peplum.

Two-piece dress with longer torso blouse.

WHAT A YEAR IT WAS!

Lavishly edged in Alençon-type lace . . . about $5.00. New longer hemline

NEW *Lacy Snow White Slip* IN DRESS SIZES

For a white Christmas—Textron's lovely new bright-white slip—of Snow White rayon satin—

three inches deep with lace!   Pretty as a snowflake and sewed with tiniest stitches.   Sized just like your dresses

to fit at the bust, waist and hip.   Just ask for your dress size . . . 12 to 20 average.

Also in Heaven Blue.   Ask to see Textron Dress Sized Slips . . . Textron-tailored from fiber

to finished fashion . . . from $3.50 to $6 at leading stores throughout the country.

TEXTRON INC., Textron Building, 401 Fifth Avenue, New York 16, N. Y.

TEXTRON
REG. U. S. PAT. OFF.

HOSTESS COATS   •   HOME FASHIONS   •   BLOUSES   •   MENSWEAR   •   LINGERIE

Let's Party

A gown to dance in made of stiff pink and gray striped taffeta. ($20)

A white moire gown with full skirt accented with red roses. ($20)

A Formal Affair

Sophisticated dinner dress with metallic blouse.

Ballet-length taffeta party dress with long sleeves.

Black jersey evening gown accented with silver belt.

we did it

...and we're glad

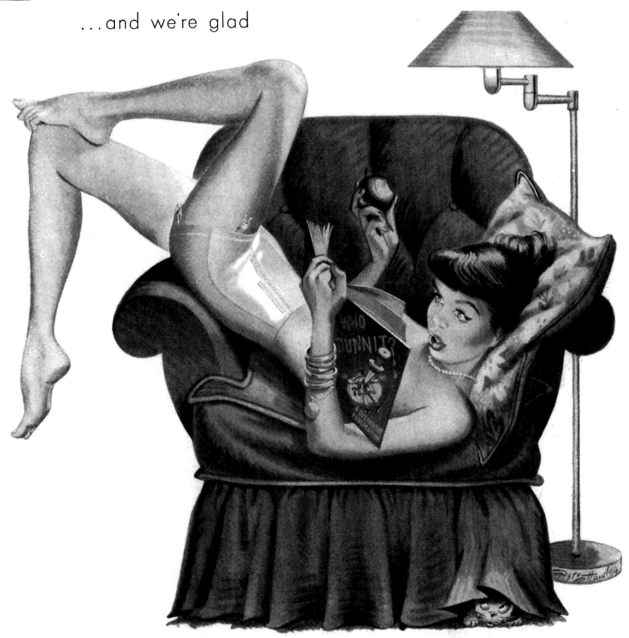

we stole it...the most wonderful control idea in the world...
from our own Jantzen swim suit designers, to be sure...
and that's why we can make Jantzen girdles and panty-girdles
so slimming, trimming, smoothing, soothing...so
light-as-air and easy-to-wear. The new Jantzens, even
more remarkable than ever, are at most stores.

* *Jantzen*

girdles
and panty-girdles
by the makers of
Jantzen swim suits

143

hair

Like Skirts Is Worn Longer With Smooth Crowns, Partly Covered Ears And Back-Of-The-Neck Flattery Resulting In A Soft, Feminine Look.

1. Swing Low. Back hair swirled smoothly down to one side, twisted firmly and pinned. End arranged in soft curls.

2. Pin-up. Very new–back hair swept up off neck to make a soft half-chignon. New, too, the big anchoring hairpin.

3. Fanfare. Lower half of back hair in fan-shaped page boy; upper half combed smoothly down with question-mark curls.

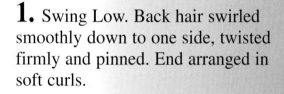

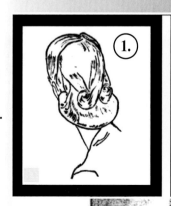
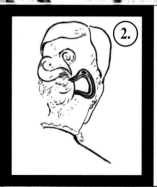
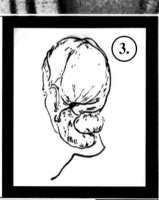

A center part with hair rolled back with forward movement at the sides.

This smooth hairstyle has flat waves and forward movement over the ears.

The hair is brought forward over the forehead.

1947

Suits

Suits Are Designed For Every Conceivable Figure And Range From Cutaways And Tunics, Boleros And Box Jackets, To Tightly Fitted And Semi-fitted Waistlines.

Suits

Suits

Long Strands Of Cultured Pearls Become Popular Again As Well As Interest In Hats Ranging From The Pillbox To The Beret With Feathers And Veils Used As Trims.

Desire For Wee Waists Spawned A New Kind Of Undergarment – Girdles Contoured To Accent Curves, Waist Bands And Boned Bodice-Brassiers To Flatten The Midriff And Cinch The Waist.

WOULDN'T IT BE GLOVERLY

GLOVES ON:

AT A RECEPTION
TEA DANCING
AT A WEDDING
SHAKING HANDS
RIDING

GLOVES OFF:

AT A TEA PARTY
AT A SOFT DRINK
  OR MILK BAR
EATING OR MUNCHING
MAKING A SPEECH
RECEIVING COMMUNION

OPTIONAL:

IN THE THEATER
DRIVING A CAR
AT THE MOVIES
TRAVELING
AT A PROM

1947

In Your Easter Bonnet

Spring Hats Are Light, Colorful And Crisp, Designed To Make Your Head Look Small And Your Neck Slender.

A grand hat accented with an oversized rose.

A closely fitting bonnet made of white straw.

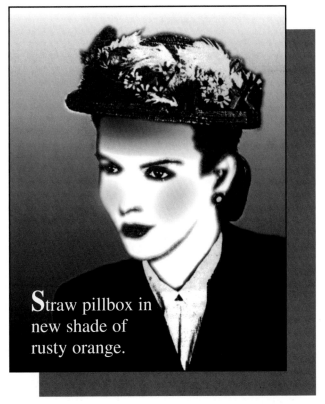

Straw pillbox in new shade of rusty orange.

Violets and turquoise velvet ribbons adorn the back of this chartreuse Milan sailor hat.

This bumper sailor made of red and white striped cotton is trimmed with white lilacs.

A huge rose sets off this small round hat with navy straw brim and red velvet crown.

A poke bonnet decorated with flowered streamers down the back.

The Price On His Head

1947

$8.00

$10.00

WHAT A YEAR IT WAS!

Bathing Suits

Despite the news from the French Riviera of a shocking new bathing suit – a tiny brassiere and a diaper drape tied on either hip, American girls stick with the traditional one-piece maillot made in white or brilliant colors and dazzling California prints.

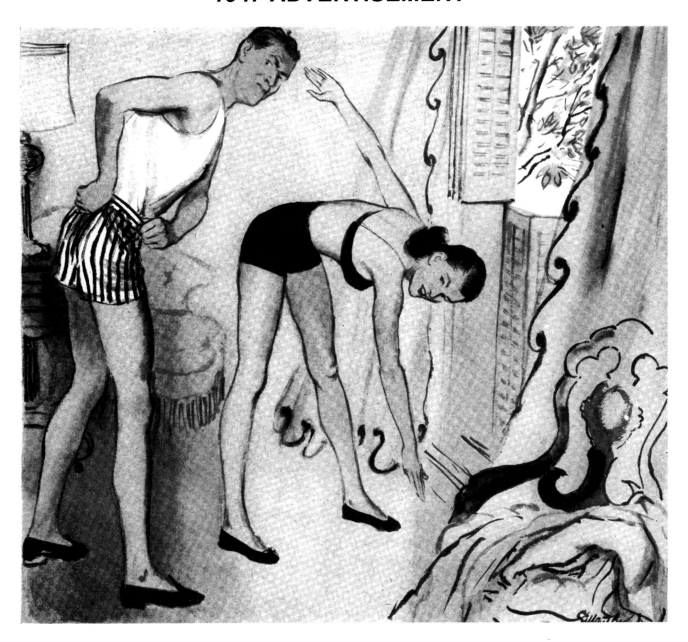

<u>Next</u> shorts, old friend, look for the "Sanforized" label →

If you don't want your shorts to become "shorter" and tighter from shrinkage, look for the "Sanforized" label *before you buy!*

Wise men (and women) *always* look for it on washable shirts, pajamas, work clothes, slacks, women's and children's wear.

The "Sanforized" label means: fabric shrinkage *held to a mere 1%.*

"Sanforized"... the checked standard of shrinkage. The "Sanforized" trade-mark is used on compressive pre-shrunk fabrics only when tests for residual shrinkage are regularly checked, through the service of the owner of the trade-mark, to insure maintenance of its established standard by users of the mark. *Cluett, Peabody & Co., Inc.*

I Could Have Danced All Night
(Not In These Shoes, Baby)

Slim Closed Opera Pump

Pump With Slashed Vamp

Open Toe Pump

Open-Shanked Sandal

Open Toe, Shut Heel

Closed Toe, Sling Heel

Open Heel, Open Toe With Butterfly Bow

Open Sandal

The Teenagers

Three-piece play suit consisting of shorts, midriff and tie-on skirt.

A black cotton eyelet-frilled dance dress.

Two-piece dress with front button blouse and pleated skirt.

WHAT A YEAR IT WAS!

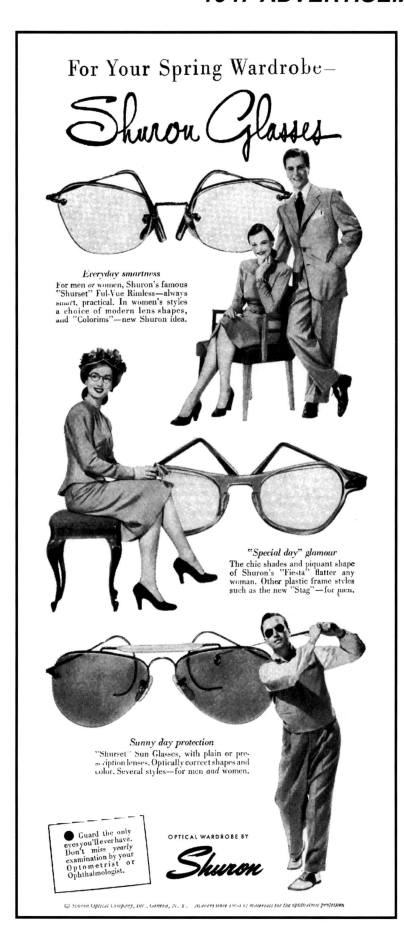

For Your Spring Wardrobe—

Shuron Glasses

Everyday smartness
For men *or* women, Shuron's famous "Shurset" Ful-Vue Rimless—always smart, practical. In women's styles a choice of modern lens shapes, and "Colorims"—new Shuron idea.

"Special day" glamour
The chic shades and piquant shape of Shuron's "Fiesta" flatter any woman. Other plastic frame styles such as the new "Stag"—for men.

Sunny day protection
"Shurset" Sun Glasses, with plain or prescription lenses. Optically correct shapes and color. Several styles—for men *and* women.

● Guard the only eyes you'll ever have. Don't miss *yearly* examination by your Optometrist or Ophthalmologist.

OPTICAL WARDROBE BY

Shuron

© Shuron Optical Company, Inc., Geneva, N. Y. Makers since 1864 of materials for the ophthalmic profession

"The best is always the cheapest"

VENIDA
The Guaranteed
HAIR NET
made of genuine human hair

- fits better
- looks better
- lasts longer

Venida's February Hair-Do looks lovely on Rhonda Fleming, under contract to Vanguard Films, producers of "Duel In The Sun," a Selznick International picture.

LOOK GLAMOROUS
In VENIDA'S February Hair-do of the Month

Write for free directions to Rieser Co., New York 18, N.Y.,— or ask your hairdresser to set it. Remember, to keep your hair-do neat and lovely all day, always wear a Venida guaranteed Hair Net. Choose the precise size, shade and shape you require.

VENIDA
Hair Beauty Aids

—include Venida Hair Nets, Hair Lacquer, Lanolin Creme Shampoo, Lanolin Hair Creme, Bobby Pins.

REMEMBER:
VENIDA RULES THE WAVES

1947 ADVERTISEMENT

Roaster Oven · Cleaner · Water Heater · Electric Sink · Refrigerator · Home Freezer · Range · Laundromat · Dryer · Radio · Mixer · Fan · Iron · Toaster · Waffle Baker · Table Grill · Warming Pad · Percolator · Comforter

THE LAST WORD IN SLEEP LUXURY!

So Beautiful, yet so Practical . . . the New Electric Comforter!

Warmth without weight . . . no other covering needed! Fall, winter, spring . . . sleep in constant, even warmth under this one *automatically controlled* Electric Comforter. Never too warm . . . never too cold, just the warmth you like best the whole night through. Made of lush, quilted rayon satin in heavenly shades of rose, blue or green. Matching underside of faille prevents slipping. Outer shell can be dry-cleaned, inner warming sheet laundered. Fits double or twin beds. Safe? *Absolutely* . . . approved by the Underwriters' Laboratories, Inc. See these Electric Comforters and other appliances at your Westinghouse retailer's now.

WESTINGHOUSE ELECTRIC CORPORATION
Plants in 25 Cities · Offices Everywhere
Appliance Division · Mansfield, Ohio

Every house needs Westinghouse
Maker of 30 MILLION Electric Home Appliances

TUNE IN *TED MALONE*
EVERY MORNING
MONDAY THROUGH FRIDAY
A B C NETWORK

158

SPORTS
Golden Gloves

In New York fight fans turn out for the Golden Gloves Tournament of Champions at Madison Square Garden.

The highlight of the evening is Johnny Stevens of New York (right) slugging it out with Emil Wilson of Pittsburgh.

In round two Stevens lands a haymaker and the lights go out for Emil Wilson.

Ringside reporters capture the exciting action.

Referee does count but Wilson doesn't stir.

Baseball

In Orlando Florida, Joe Tinker holds baseball school.

Ben Kentwell, of the Braves, leads pitching practice.

Future hopefuls practice their sliding technique.

WHAT A YEAR IT WAS!

School

Local citrus beauties are brought in to break the intensity of training.

Pretty girls and baseball—what a tough life.

And now for some tips on how to swing.

Baseball

JACKIE ROBINSON Breaks 80-Year Old Color Barrier And Becomes The First Negro* To Sign A Contract With A Major Baseball Club

Boston Red Sox Outfielder Ted Williams Wins Second Triple Crown For Batting, Home Runs And Runs Batted In.

Alan Roth Becomes Baseball's First Statistician As He Goes To Work For The Brooklyn Dodgers.

Famous Births

Johnny Bench
Nolan Ryan

Passings

Negro Baseball League's **Josh Gibson**, negro* baseball's greatest home run hitter, dies at age 35 after a 17-year career and 960 homers.

	NATIONAL LEAGUE	AMERICAN LEAGUE
PLAYER OF THE YEAR	Bob Elliot, *Boston Braves*	Joe DiMaggio, *New York Yankees*
ROOKIE OF THE YEAR	Jackie Robinson, *Brooklyn Dodgers*	*None Designated*
SEASON HOME RUN KINGS	Ralph Kiner, *Pittsburgh Pirates* Johnny Mize, *New York Giants*	Ted Williams, *Boston Red Sox*
SEASON BATTING CHAMPS	Harry Walker, *Philadelphia Phillies*	Ted Williams, *Boston Red Sox*
MOST VALUABLE PLAYER	Bob Elliott, *Boston Braves*	Joe DiMaggio, *New York Yankees*

*Negro was the commonly-used term in 1947.

New York Yankees Edge Brooklyn Dodgers 4-3, Winning World Series

Brooklyn Dodgers Manager, Leo Durocher, Suspended For Full Season For Personal Infractions Deemed Detrimental To Baseball.

WHAT A YEAR IT WAS!

NEW YORK GIANTS 1947

The New York Giants report to Phoenix for Spring Training.

Cliff Hartug (left), prize rookie, is expected to do big things for the Giants this coming season.

Walker Cooper will be behind the plate when they yell "Play Ball."

The team does a little warming up in the Arizona sun.

Brooklyn Dodgers

Leo Durocher and Branch Rickey supervise Spring Training in Havana for the Brooklyn Dodgers.

Leo caught in a happy moment.

The pitching staff lines up for throwing practice.

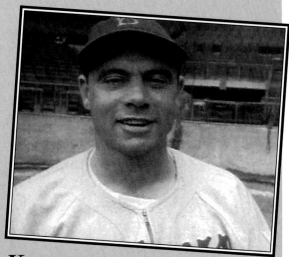

Kirby Higby is once again slated to be part of the pitching staff this season.

The infielders line up and wait for instruction.

All-Star Pee Wee Reese is assured of his old spot at shortstop.

Pete Reiser practices his swing.

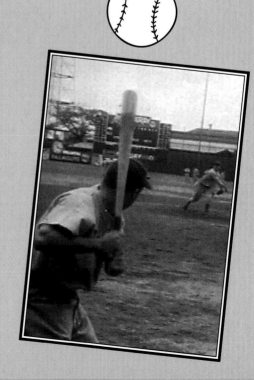

Dixie Walker shares the secrets of his success with his teammates.

Those "Bums" are looking real good!

THIS YEAR GIVE WISELY— *Give Norge!*

Only Norge has automatic defrosting!

Electric cookery at its best!

Zero-store and save more!

Now you'll always be in hot water!

Clothes come cleaner, last longer!

Something new in gas ranges!

Home is where the heat is!

There's great satisfaction—great *comfort*—in owning or in *giving* a Norge appliance. For a Norge performs its appointed task so well that it rapidly becomes "one of the family." Each Norge product—electric range, refrigerator, washer, gas range, home heater, home freezer and electric water heater—has exclusive features which distinguish it from the average . . . . lift it from the commonplace. So shop wisely this year, for yourself and for others. . . . "The best dealer in town sells Norge" and you will find him listed in the classified section of your telephone book. Norge Division, Borg-Warner Corporation, Detroit 26, Michigan.

Norge products, distributed worldwide, are typical examples of the values made possible by the American system of free enterprise.

SEE
NORGE
BEFORE YOU BUY

Products of BORG-WARNER

BW

REFRIGERATORS • ELECTRIC RANGES • WASHERS • ELECTRIC WATER HEATERS • GAS RANGES • HOME HEATERS • HOME & FARM FREEZERS

BOXING

Welterweight Champ SUGAR RAY ROBINSON (Walker Smith) Knocks Out JIMMY DOYLE In The 8th Round. Doyle Dies Of His Injuries Next Day.

•

Heavyweight Champion JOE LOUIS Beats Jersey JOE WALCOTT On A Split Decision.

RACING

MAN O'WAR, Considered The Greatest Horse Of The First Half Of The 20th Century, Dies. Winning 20 Out Of 21 Races, After Retirement The Stallion Sired 383 Foals.

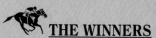 **THE WINNERS**

KENTUCKY DERBY
"Jet Pilot"- Eric Guerin, Jockey
PREAKNESS
"Faultless"- Doug Dodson, Jockey
BELMONT STAKES
"Phalanx"- R. Donso, Jockey
HORSE OF THE YEAR
"Armed"- Calumet Farm, Owner

GOLF

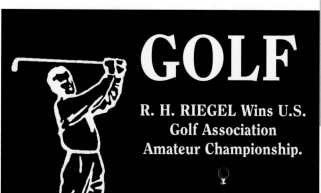

R. H. RIEGEL Wins U.S. Golf Association Amateur Championship.

LEW WORSHAM Wins U.S. Open.

FRED DALY Takes British Open.

JIMMY DEMARET Wins U.S. Masters.

MILDRED "BABE" DIDRICKSON ZAHARIAS First Woman To Win British Open.

WHAT A YEAR IT WAS!

HOCKEY

Toronto Maple Leafs Beat Montreal Canadiens 4-2 Winning Stanley Cup.

ROOKIE OF THE YEAR HOWIE MEEKER, Toronto Maple Leafs

1947 ADVERTISEMENT

SAVATE

The French call it *Savate* or *Kick Boxing* or *I Get A Kick Out Of You.*

What are you kicking about? It hurts me more than it does you.

WHAT A YEAR IT WAS!

It's *Smart*
to own
an Olds

The coat—a new All-Weather Topper by Duchess Royal. The car—a new "98" 4-Door Sedan by Oldsmobile.

It's *Smart* to go automatic ...

Takes more than a spring shower to dim the beauty of this big new 1947 Oldsmobile. It's smart in appearance ... it's smooth in performance ... come rain or shine. Fact is, when wet weather slows down the traffic, that's when you really appreciate driving without shifting gears or pushing a clutch—the Hydra-Matic way. It's safer, too, because GM Hydra-Matic Drive* gives smoother power under perfect control — *automatically!* No wonder so many *smart* people choose Oldsmobile this year!

(White sidewall tires at extra cost when available.)

Oldsmobile

OFFERING

GM
GENERAL
MOTORS

HYDRA-MATIC
DRIVE

*Optional at extra cost

St. Johns Beats University Of Hawaii

The University Of Hawaii basketball team comes to New York's Madison Square Garden to compete against the favored St. Johns' quintet.

A sell-out crowd of enthusiastic fans show up to root for their favorite team.

In their first mainland appearance, the previously unbeaten Hawaiian team has a considerable height disadvantage.

Of the 14 St. Johns' team members used during the game, all but one scored with St. Johns winning by a score of 80 to 37.

WHAT A YEAR IT WAS!

Rootin' for the Big Five— Cinco

At Madison Square Garden — New York

Smooth co-ordination on the court makes five stars a great team. Smooth blending of five features makes Cinco a great smoke. A favorite of all ages, Cinco is gaining more and more applause from the younger set who have come to know a good cigar when they smoke one! The five big features put more pleasure in every puff.

CINCO MEANS FIVE

1 Havana—*gives Cinco aroma.*

2 Puerto Rican—*gives it flavor and mildness.*

3 Broadleaf—*gives it mellowness.*

4 Shadegrown—*gives it character.*

5 100% long filler—*makes it burn slowly, evenly.*

A PRODUCT OF THE WEBSTER TOBACCO COMPANY, INC., N. Y.

THAT GOOD AMERICAN CIGAR

ADV. BY N. W. AYER

11¢

171

1947

FOOTBALL

Illinois Trounces UCLA 45-14, Winning The Rose Bowl

Army Whips Navy 21-0

Chicago Cardinals Beat Philadelphia Eagles 28-21 Winning NFL Championship

HEISMAN TROPHY WINNER John Lujack, Notre Dame Quarterback

TENNIS

U.S Defeats Australia 4-1 To Win Davis Cup.

U.S. Women Win Wightman Cup In 7-0 Sweep In Forest Hills.

U.S. OPEN TENNIS ASSOCIATION SINGLES CHAMPIONSHIP

Men: Jack Kramer
         (over Frank Parker)

Women: Louise Brough
         (over Margaret Osborne)

WIMBLEDON

Men: Jack Kramer
         (over Tom Brown)

Women: Margaret Osborne
         (over Doris Hart)

WHAT A YEAR IT WAS!

ICE SKATING

WORLD FIGURE SKATING CHAMPIONSHIP

Men: **Dick Button (U.S.)**

Women: **Barbara Ann Scott (Canada)**
First North American woman to win championship

U.S. NATIONAL

Men: **Dick Button (U.S.)**

Women: **Gretchen Merrill**

CANADIAN NATIONAL

Men: **Norris F. Bowden**

Women: **Marilyn Ruth Take**

Famous Births

Kareem Abdul-Jabbar
O.J. Simpson

AUTO RACING

British racing driver, JOHN DOBB, establishes world ground speed record of 394.196 miles per hour.

•

MAURI ROSE wins 31st annual Indy 500 with speed averaging 116.3 MPH.

BASKETBALL

BASKETBALL ASSOCIATION OF AMERICA
Philadelphia Warriors over Chicago Stags 83-80, winning 4 games to 1.

•

Holy Cross beats Oklahoma University 58-47 taking National Collegiate Athletic Association Championship.

CYCLING

JEAN ROBIC, French racer, wins post-war Tour de France.

ATHLETE OF THE YEAR

Male
Johnny Lujack (football)

Female
Mildred "Babe" Didrickson Zaharias (golf)

WHAT A YEAR IT WAS!

1947 WAS A GREAT YEAR, BUT....

THE BEST IS YET TO COME!